Narcissism Book of Quotes

*A SELECTION OF QUOTES FROM
THE COLLECTIVE WISDOM
OF OVER 12,000 INDIVIDUAL DISCUSSIONS*

"I was married to a Narcissist for 16 years.
It's the closest thing there is to
HELL ON EARTH."

There have been well over 12,000 individual discussions posted at the Suite 101 Narcissistic Personality Disorder Discussion site over the past 18 months. In the preparation of this document, we encountered victim's reports of attempted murders, physical assault requiring hospitalization, mental abuse requiring hospitalization and medication that span many years, severe financial loss and consequences, stalking, workplace bullying and harassment, sexual abuse, incest, vindictiveness in child custody court battles, repudiation of pension contracts, and non-payment of child-support, all as a result of involvement with persons with Narcissistic Personality Disorder. For obvious reasons these quotes cannot be used. For equally obvious reasons, what has been inflicted upon them cannot be ignored.

The Editors

Acknowledgement

I would like to express my appreciation to the hundreds of posters who contribute at this discussion site, and to those who participated in producing this document.

Sam Vaknin

CONTENTS

<u>Narcissistic Personality Disorder</u>

<u>The Narcissistic Predator</u>

<u>Oh, What a Tangled Web They Weave</u>
<u>Lies, Lies and More Lies</u>

<u>Reclaiming Sanity: Understanding, Coping, Boundaries</u>

<u>On the Funny Side of the Street</u>
<u>... (Our Blunders, Bloopers, Typos, One-liners and Jokes)</u>

<u>Random Quotes</u>

<u>Links and Resources</u>

Abbreviations Used:

N   = Narcissist, Narcissism
NS   = Narcissistic Supply (the attention, admiration Ns want)
NPD = Narcissistic Personality Disorder
PD   = Personality Disorder

Narcissistic Personality Disorder

An all-pervasive pattern of grandiosity (in fantasy or behaviour), need for admiration or adulation and lack of empathy, usually beginning by early adulthood and present in various contexts. Five (or more) of the following criteria must be met:
- Feels grandiose and self-importance (e.g., exaggerates achievements and talents to the point of lying, demands to be recognised as superior without commensurate achievements);
- Is obsessed with fantasies of unlimited success, fame, fearsome power or omnipotence, unequalled brilliance (the cerebral narcissist), bodily beauty or sexual performance (the somatic narcissist), or ideal, everlasting, all-conquering love or passion;
- Firmly convinced that he or she is unique and, being special, can only be understood by, should only be treated by, or associate with, other special or unique, or high-status people (or institutions);
- Requires excessive admiration, adulation, attention and affirmation – or, failing that, wishes to be feared and to be notorious (Narcissistic Supply);
- Feels entitled. Expects unreasonable or special and favourable priority treatment. Demands automatic and full compliance with his or her expectations;
- Is "interpersonally exploitative", i.e., uses others to achieve his or her own ends;
- Devoid of empathy. Is unable or unwilling to identify with or acknowledge the feelings and needs of others;
- Constantly envious of others or believes that they feel the same about him or her;
- Arrogant, haughty behaviours or attitudes coupled with rage when frustrated, contradicted, or confronted.

Summarised from:

American Psychiatric Association (2000). Diagnostic and Statistical Manual of Mental Disorders, fourth edition, text revision (DSM-IV-TR). Washington, DC: American Psychiatric Association.

Malignant Self Love - Narcissism Revisited by: Sam Vaknin, Narcissus Publications, Skopje and Prague, 1999-2006.

http://samvak.tripod.com/npdglance.html

Return

The Narcissistic Predator

"The narcissist inflicts pain and abuse on others. He devalues Sources of Supply, callously and off-handedly abandons them, and discards people, places, partnerships, and friendships unhesitatingly. Sudden shifts between sadism and altruism, abuse and 'love', ignoring and caring, abandoning and clinging, viciousness and remorse, the harsh and the tender - are, perhaps, the most difficult to comprehend and to accept. These swings produce in people around the narcissist emotional insecurity, an eroded sense of self worth, fear, stress, and anxiety ('walking on eggshells'). Gradually, emotional paralysis ensues and they come to occupy the same emotional wasteland inhabited by the narcissist, his prisoners and hostages in more ways than one - and even when he is long out of their life."

Article: Other People's Pain by Sam Vaknin
http://www.suite101.com/article.cfm/npd/76632

"The brutal change in him was all the more shocking because of what he had appeared to be. The devaluation was indescribable, unnerving, frightening. His N rages used to burst forth several times a day. I found I was married to a total stranger, a Jekyll and Hyde who sometimes looked at me as if he didn't even know me. Exhausting is an understatement - it was like clinging to the edge of a cliff 24 hours a day."

"I suppose you can tell I'm scared. I believe I will end up either dead or in a mental hospital very soon if something drastic doesn't happen. He is so diabolical and so convincing to other people that my own family has abandoned me. My kids have also been brainwashed, something I would have bet my life could never happen. All of my financial means have been exhausted. Child support should have been more than enough to make it until I could finish my degree, but he quit his job to keep me from having money, and no matter what I try to do, I hit a big brick wall."

"The night he dumped me, the last thing he said to me before wandering out was 'protect yourself'. I've always puzzled over exactly what he meant, and those words have come back to haunt me now – that warning to get away from him. Without a doubt, the worst had yet to come..."

"Narcissists are great con-artists. After all, they succeed in deluding themselves! As a result, very few professionals see through them."

"I keep stressing that people with NPD do not present with the traits of their disorder. Far from it. How could any normal person take up with someone who had his NPD traits on show at the outset of a relationship? I suppose my husband had lots of practice, and had his supply-hunting tactics down to a fine art. This is the case with the real thing, full-blown NPD."

"Where would these Ns be without women, kids and the elderly to pick on?"

"I feel like I have extricated myself from a cult."

"I stood there thinking: 'He can't mean it'. I had the shudders, my skin was crawling. This N-from-hell exuded pure evil. Over the next 5 years he kicked his father out of the house, cut off his pension and slandered him. He cheated his first wife and his kids of money he should have paid, manipulated his business(s), lied to his separate little groups, split away from former friends and family, got 'religion', verbally abused his kids, turned other people into his little evil-doer proxies, hired and fired people on a regular basis. He'd cheat himself to satisfy his own greed if he could. About every three months I'd hear about some treachery he was inflicting on someone, somewhere."

"They think they are untouchable, inhabitants of a special world, one parallel to ours but never touching. Outlandish behaviour is the N's hallmark. They can draw other unsuspecting, and usually respectable, people into their criminal or pseudo-criminal activities."

"N's count on our shame to keep their secrets. They know that exposing them means exposing our own failings. That's what makes them so powerful. They manipulate us into these situations then sit back and watch us squirm between protecting ourselves or blowing the whistle."

"You have to live through the horror of the N experience to be able to understand it. People say: 'But he's mad about you'. The only pertinent word in that sentence is 'mad'."

"The relationship with the N was too good to be true. They want something from you. When you finally wake up and confront them on their bad behaviour, it's something you do, for yourself. You get it off your chest. When the N asks how you are doing, they are taking your emotional temperature to see if you are reacting, because they are looking for that reaction from you. When you finally give them a piece of your mind, they're not even listening. It goes in one ear and out the other. They sit, rather impassively, appearing like they are taking it in, but if you do a test, you find that they were not listening at all, because they can not quote back to you, anything you said. So consider that action as an exercise for yourselves. Nothing you will ever say to that person will make a difference."

"Yes I told him exactly what I think of him, his lies, his deceit, his lack of emotions, he is just an image not a real person ... and I realise that not only did this not bother him, it actually made him feel great! He knows that he has a dramatic impact on my feelings and since he won't let me love him anymore, now he makes me hate him. This must really make him feel like he's one damn special and unforgettable person!"

"I went back to him a dozen times, each time somehow thinking it was different, that maybe now that we had addressed all the issues and brought everything into the open, and he admitted he had treated me badly ... it would change. And it WOULD go back to (almost) how it had been, but each time that honeymoon period would last a shorter and shorter amount of time. It absolutely wrecked me – my self-esteem has never been lower than during my years with him."

"But these qualities, are indeed 'charm'. The proof of the power of this brand of charm is that you, and I, both women who are probably reasonably alert, failed to see through this well-constructed mask."

"Maybe it is bad for me to wish her unfortunate times, but, that is what she deserves. I have never met anyone more evil than she is. It's the kind of evil that masquerades as good."

"It was the losing of myself that caused me the most anguish. I could feel it, like a brain washing, like a vampire, and he claimed he didn't know anything was wrong, didn't know what I meant when I said I was sad all the time and couldn't trust a word he said."

"I have always felt like they did this on purpose - like they were the most cunning people I've encountered to orchestrate all this turmoil, but through this Web site, I've come to learn that I'm wrong and that there truly are deeper reasons an N acts out like they do. The key for you is to learn as much as you can as fast as you can, and protect yourself financially and emotionally. Not too many people survive the devastation of a tornado."

"NPD is actually quite simple. When they want supply (adoration/veneration) they put on the whole show to obtain that supply. As the supply wanes, because no one can sustain all the time that high-octane adoration the N requires, then the N begins to get uneasy and devaluation sets in, followed by confusion and bewilderment on the part of the spouse/partner, who thinks s/he has done everything 'right'."

"In order to overcome one's enemy, one must study diligently to understand how he came to be your enemy, what his motivations and goals are. Fully understanding your enemy and then rational planning based on that knowledge is the only way to emerge the victor. We are learning about those with Narcissistic Personality Disorder, Antisocial Personality Disorder, Borderline Personality Disorder, Histrionic Personality Disorder, as well as those with Sadistic and/or Masochistic Personality Disorder - the psychopaths in our lives, learning to defend ourselves against their destructive forces and how to avoid them in the future."

"I read Sam Vaknin's book first, that's when I finally knew it wasn't me for the first time. Knowledge is power, know everything you can about narcissism."

"I raise a glass to all the other warriors on here, and to Sam Vaknin too, for providing this forum, and so much useful information. His writings are powerful and painful, and marked the first turning on the road for me. I can remember reading and re-reading the FAQs in a mesmerised daze, as I saw my experience and the disaster that is NPD unfold in black on white before my eyes."

"The withdrawal from my N has been terrible and hard on me but it is getting better. I no longer have anger and rage and my mind is settling down. And I no longer think of him 24 hours of the day. I never thought that would ever happen just a couple of months ago."

"I loved him, very much, but no way was I about to be obsessed. I also lived for my work, for myself, for all manner of things, friends and family included. This, the N cannot take at all, and will try to drive in that wedge, in order to get ALL attention for himself."

"My ex-N would constantly talk about himself. Every type of conversation, somehow always came back to him talking about him. It would be embarrassing, when friends would need to talk about something happening in their lives, he could not listen, or be supportive. He never got it. He would quickly turn the conversation back to himself."

"The other thing he did was leave me in all kinds of situations to go find someone to charm. If we went to social things, he would not talk to me all night. He would need to be the centre of attention in some group. Usually women."

"He will have a new female N supplier ASAP and you can bet he'll be parading her in front of you too."

"I wish I could offer you any encouragement with your NPD/Bi-polar loved one, but in the 11 years I've dealt with them in my life, I've only known grief, lies, distorted realities, schemes, police, chaos, courts. I often feel like they sit in the eye of a self-created tornado and watch their loved ones circling around in total chaos, and if the winds ever die down, they find a way to get them whirling again."

"My ex-girlfriend seemed for nearly six years to be a kind, caring, supportive person ... and then did a 180. Trashing me and, trashing (it turned out) at least one other person that I know of. Extremely rude and cruel behaviour, calculated to cause me extreme pain."

"If you want something to cry about, cry for the N's new victim(s), the innocent, unmarked, un-inoculated prey. The victims are carefully chosen, and I feel sad for them."

"In fact I didn't even realise how badly he was abusing me. I didn't know that all of the silent treatments I got and the alienation from my friends and family were all forms of abuse. Which made me even feel more victimised when I put two and two together."

"The abuse doesn't happen because the victims volunteer for it. The abuse happens because the abusers lie, manipulate and speak in mixed messages, and out of love and a sense of fairness we trust them."

"Towards the end of my relationship with N, he told me: 'Your father couldn't break your spirit, and as hard as I've tried, neither can I'. About sums it all up wouldn't you say?"

"He would tell women he loved them all at the same time, keeping each woman separate from the others, trying to get one of them to marry him."

"She said she was like a recorder that took everything in and reported it just like a recorder. What I was slowly realising was that yes, she was like a machine - a recorder that took the info in, twisted, spun it into whatever, and then used it as a weapon to stir up controversy or create problems."

"The N has no feeling of any kind, you must absolutely remember that. Any 'feelings' or emotions shown are like those put on by an actor on stage. They look good, but are only an act."

"The person with NPD is unpredictable, that is part of the disorder. Their world is a heaving, restless, unquiet place, full of anxieties and unknown quantities. And when they withdraw the 'caring' and the 'loving' and start on the devaluation stage, then the contrast is so appalling that we are wrecked, unable to understand (at this stage most of us had never heard of NPD) so naturally we thought we were at fault in some way."

"When I met my N I thought I had just met the most wonderful person ever born! Nice, kind, talented, intelligent, even caring and concerned. It wasn't until a few months had passed that I began to feel something wasn't right and I was confused. I felt like I was on the verge of a nervous breakdown but couldn't put my finger on the problem (because I thought it was me) until I came here. I still can't figure out what the telltale signs were that I apparently missed. It took a long time for the confusion to build up. And I still haven't had the courage that a lot of you have had to make the complete break."

"You cannot understand his mind, the disordered mind, because you are normal. How could you? You can believe it – he is not real, and nothing is real to him. That is his tragedy."

"As I said, it is only lately that I heard about how she hates him to this day, after twenty years or more."

"Anyway, the uneasy was always there for me too. It was just easy to ignore in the beginning. As I got to know him, the uneasiness shifted to a feeling of walking on eggshells since I never knew what action or word I might do would trip over one of his innumerable emotional landmines."

"I made a huge mistake today. After receiving the latest personal assault from my N, I tried to arrange an amicable settlement without having to go to court. My biggest concern was that he not get overnight visitation. Well, he agreed to my terms and our lawyers placed a conference call to the judge to adjourn our 'motion'. Soon after that, my N backed out of the whole deal saying he didn't see why he shouldn't have our child overnight. Now we don't go to court for another 3 months!! They will use anything and everything at their disposal."

"He is a very insecure (and jealous) man, but he is also a dreadful coward. The Ns usually are."

"If some man were to say to your daughter: 'Here's the deal, sweetie. For several months or so, I'm going to pretend to be everything you ever wanted. I'll shower you with attention, affection and all manner of stuff to make you feel special. Then, once I know you're depending on me as your significant other, and have made a commitment, I'm going to quit pretending and be who I really am. I'm going to start treating you really badly, I'll say insensitive things, I'll lie, I'll cheat, I'll be really cruel, possibly humiliate you in public. Hey, I might even beat you. Your job will be to figure out what happened and do everything in your power to restore the relationship to what it was, until you either die, try to kill yourself, or collapse and get sent to hospital, which will be pretty funny because there's no chance whatsoever I'll ever pretend to be that 'nice guy' again – and by the way, it WAS a pretence. So what do you say, sweetie? Do we have a deal? Several years of hell in exchange for a few months of fantasy?'

If your daughter whipped out the pen to ink the deal, you'd smack her and say, 'What are you, NUTS? This guy's a lunatic!!!' Right? But that IS the deal. That is the contract. If that contract wouldn't be nearly good enough for your daughter, why would it be good enough for you?"

"I went along with him once and he said: 'Hey I like the way you talk!!!' He actually praised me when I agreed with him that a person who causes an accident should be left on the highway to die and just drive on by. What a polished piece of work! I swear I met the devil."

"What I'm wondering right now is ... in the beginning when he was treating me like a Queen, was there a hidden agenda there? Was it always in the back of his mind that he would soon unleash the hidden fury to hurt me? He acts like I am 'the one', the 'kindred friend' that he's never had before. Is this all a lie? I seem to be hanging on to the hope that it will be different for me. Am I fooling myself?"

"Does he want to hurt you? Well, now, that would imply that he thinks of you as a human being - an N doesn't. What he wants is to secure supply. If he cannot do it by means of flattery, he will do it by means of cruelty. The goal is to get you to give him what he wants. He doesn't especially care which method he uses, so long as he finds one that works. I know that sounds cold. It is cold. That is the mind of a narcissist. Cold and devoid of empathy. Because he lacks empathy, he probably doesn't know or care if he hurts you, unless he's using bullying as a technique for extracting NS from you. Even then, he couldn't care less what that does to you, apart from eliciting the desired response. If it makes him feel better about himself to belittle you, he will do that, but the ultimate goal isn't to make you feel bad, the goal is perpetuate the myth of his own perfection and simultaneously control you. If by hurting you it gets you in check, makes you take on his failings as your own, and make you work twice as hard for his approval, it's a bonus for him. If he doesn't need to employ cruelty in order to accomplish either of the above goals, he won't. It's that simple."

"Who would not assume s/he was so lucky to have met this wonderful, caring individual. Nothing wrong with that. It is when the cannon-ball of devaluation hits you that the horror of the situation begins to dawn, but you cannot work out why. Naturally, you assume (because you think within normal parameters) that your partner/spouse is ill, has encountered a serious problem (work, finances), is maybe physically ill. Because you have never heard of NPD you do not, indeed cannot, know about the idealisation-devaluation process."

"The N I write about probably never did a thing, unless there was something in it for him. He simply did not bother. He started from a position of weakness, in that he had a huge inferiority complex, but the pretentiousness of his facade gave the impression of enormous self-confidence."

"My N also had very low self-esteem. It was as if he had to constantly bolster himself up to me by references to past relationships, and present/future possibilities. He always made me feel like I just didn't match up. Now I realise that probably no one ever could have. He was always looking for such an amount of NS that no normal person/relationship could have possibly have supplied it, and I think that insecurity was also behind the need to have, ideally, lots of different alternatives."

"It is THEM, not you or I, who can't trust enough to invest/try/be content with one relationship and build on that. The lack of commitment, sneaky manipulation of targeting new NS, guarantee that they will get dumped by anybody decent - lowering their self-esteem even further. But they seem to hurl compulsively along the same tired worn-out path."

"I had to analyse him closely and that's what saved me. I drew up a list of things he had done, sat down with my therapist and discussed what those behaviours/symptoms were, from a psychological perspective. We were like 2 scientists, working on a project, where there wasn't a lot of documentation to refer to. Ultimately we identified narcissism, but went further. We wound up with the diagnosis that, not only was he a psychopath, he was also a sociopath, as he had no conscience."

"Diagnosing Ns truly isn't rocket science. Go through the list of criteria. Give an example beside each one stating why s/he's like that. When you get 5 or more, BINGO. It's the stories, the anecdotal reports that diagnose Ns. My N fully met the criteria for 4 different PDs, plus bipolar. He went to a psychiatrist only once, about 16 years ago. He's a successful businessman and he's a narcissistic psychopath."

"In actual fact, it was the doctor who diagnosed my husband who remarked on the high incidence of NPD among prison inmates, i.e. among the criminal population. This same doctor is also a prison psychologist working for the State, (as well as a university lecturer)."

"Yes, absolutely. It's not a disorder of intelligence. Far from it. My N graduated law school near the top of his class. Emotionally, he's 5 years old!!!"

"He told me that based on what he has read in my journals and narratives, providing that all the information is correct (which it is) that my N is a psychopath, narcissist and borderline. I was shocked that he thought it was more than narcissism. So, I am interpreting it to mean that a person with Multiple Personality Disorder tendencies will exhibit some of the characteristics from each, but not necessarily all of them."

"On first meeting an N, what is it that they do, that a normal person does not do? From the perspective of the one who is meeting the N for the first time, a N goes to great lengths to make a big impression on the listener. The N never stops doing that. They want to be sure they have your attention and they will appear to be listening very attentively, as you speak. The listening attentively part is an illusion. If questioned about the discussion later, they will not remember a word that was said. Reason: They were too busy studying you. What you care about. They make such observations to use against you, later on."

"It is best to keep them at arm's length and not even start a relationship with someone who is too much 'over the top', in every way. They leave a path of destruction and dozens of broken hearts, in their wake. Sometimes, the damage cannot be undone and you must live with it. So beware of someone who is coming on too strong."

"We have a saying around my house which is that an N will put you through a series of increasingly difficult (and more ludicrous) tests in order to get you to prove loyalty to them. If you manage to pass all of these ridiculous tests, you are rewarded for your considerable effort with the right to worship the N. I don't know about anyone else, but I've got other plans."

"I have come to think of those years as a classroom in which I learned about my own vulnerabilities. Nothing seems as scary to me anymore ... how can it be when I have survived living with, as Sam Vaknin has said, an encounter with 'the first carbon-based form of artificial intelligence'."

"I had never known a real conman in my life. I thought only the stupid or elderly got suckered."

"What I, and others on this board, have learned from dealing with N bullies in our personal lives, applies to terrorists. There can be no appeasement, no attempting to reason with them, no attempt to "fix" them, to unseat their deep-seated hatred, shame and envy. Sounds terribly harsh to the uninitiated, but not recognising that can only lead to our own destruction."

"I've come to believe that, to the N, the world looks like a place where the only food is meat and we're the cattle. That's why, at the most primitive level, they think they 'have to' act the way they do in order to survive. They've got a vested interest in suppressing that empathy. At a fundamental level, WE ARE NOT REAL to them. Do you ever wonder if your hamburger had a name? You and I are interchangeable cows to them. Stings a little, right? Yes, they're accountable, all right. They try to mutilate us for meat! Once we get over the shock that THAT THERE REALLY ARE PEOPLE LIKE THIS IN THE WORLD, our sense of survival kicks in and we get out before they slaughter us wholesale. Arguing with them about the reality of their perceptions is pointless; it won't stop them from hacking off a piece of meat. The damage they do is real, but don't expect them to ever understand that, not on a gut level where it counts for you and me. You want to get even with the N? Take away the meat."

"They mix people up by screwing up the issues up so we get confused. Then they reprioritise everything for us by getting angry so we have to look at them first, we think and we worry about them first. It becomes all about them. Everything else, especially ourselves and things once important to us becomes second fiddle. No wonder we feel something isn't right and we don't realise how we got ourselves into such a predicament."

"Like you, I have the 'I hope he gets his just desserts' thoughts. But there'll always be someone they can fool. (In my ex-N's case, aged 45, I see he's homed in on a 20 year old who he 'helps' with her exams, I hope she's astute enough to suss him out, but who knows?). The really true sign we've recovered completely is that we won't harbour thoughts about what they're doing to whom – not care – or at least accept that it's out of our control. Do we really care about the 'others' – or – and I hold my hand up here, are we perhaps not more enraged that they're still 'getting away' with it!?"

"I was married for several years to a man who exhibited this precise pattern. It ultimately ended in a domestic violence situation and after great struggle, I left him. The act of leaving him brought further abuse and grievances."

"I guess the reality is that even when it seems so completely innocent, there's always an ulterior motive running through their minds. It blows me away that every event in their lives, no matter how significant or insignificant, can always be used to create the turmoil that seems to constantly surround them."

"Your post evoked a memory of yet another conversation I had with my ex-N. I had referred to sex as making love. She looked at me very inquisitively and said: 'I noticed you say that a lot – why do you call it making love?' So, I replied: 'Why, what would you call it?' Her response was: 'I would just call it SEX. I'm not really sure what LOVE is!' Looking back, it was yet another obvious NPD zinger that zinged right by me."

"Almost four years and he didn't know my birthday or my full name! It's their way of saying 'you don't matter that much to me'."

"Pretend you are someone other than yourself looking into what's going on in your head. It helps me because it detaches me somehow and I can see things clearer when looking at it in a different perspective."

"We cannot accurately predict what response we will get on any given day. And without the ability to predict – without a stable system on which we can rely – we wind up tying ourselves into knots trying desperately to please and walking on eggshells hoping to avoid this unpredictable wrath."

"It is excruciating pain. It is the pain of separation, the pain of loss, the pain of dreams and expectations unrealised. It is the loss and death of a mirage."

"He chose every path less likely to cause him any disruption in his routine, without giving one ounce of thought of the retributions of his acts. And whenever asked for an explanation the response was always the same... It was someone else's fault or, if there was no one else to point the finger of blame to, he 'couldn't remember' the event in question, or he was just feeling bad that day."

"In my case N, husband of 12 years, is not exactly malicious. He doesn't set out to hurt me just for kicks, in my opinion. He hurts me as little or as much as it takes to achieve his goal: to make me dependant on him in as many ways, obey him, give him all the NS he demands, abdicate control. So, while his primary goal isn't to hurt me, it becomes a goal if that's what it takes to get NS out of me."

"Through my self-education I've experienced opposite ends of emotion. On one hand it's been enlightening, cleansing, joyous, and uplifting. On the other hand it's been revolting, heart-achingly painful, gut-wrenchingly toxic, and horribly embarrassing."

"After finding this group, as much as I have been comforted, I have also been disturbed by the hurt that all of us have survived thus far at the hand of an N. I think I might still be in shock that my N, a human being, is actually capable of hurting another so much, with no remorse – except when it impacts him."

"One of the very difficult things to deal with after being the victim of a N is that most people will not want to believe what happened to you, even if they saw it with their own eyes!"

"The point is, I was getting sick and mad, was losing weight and concentration at work... I'm the typical co-dependent, I know ... and I really thought the power of love would help."

"Sam Vaknin's article Other People's Pain is well worth reading right now. It's like a bucket of ice water when we need it to remind ourselves what this is all about."

"I guess the computer is a screen for Ns – they can present themselves anyway they want and be exactly what you say, someone's prince charming. The e-card that I found from his last affair had her saying: 'I can't wait to make you happy for the rest of my life and give you the love you deserve!' UGH! I can't even imagine what bag of goods he sold her."

"I too became lost in HIS world, started walking on eggshells and worrying if I said or was behaving the right way for him. He was so methodical in his control over me and like you, he would throw a bone at me (usually some old flowers on their way out), and I like a jerk would get so excited that he thought a little about me with the award of almost dead flowers. So sad."

"I remember asking tons of people if he ever made eye contact with them. This was before I knew anything about NPD, but I knew there was something very, very wrong with him. EVERYONE said

NO, without hesitation – it was as if they had all thought about that very thing, or at least had noticed it independently. Creepy."

"I learned that 'kicking you when you're down' is a standard characteristic of the N."

"I told him no more because he was making me feel horrible, but the fact that he accepted it so easily hurts all the more. It validates just how meaningless all of it was and is. I was feeling OK and suddenly it's all hit me again like a ton of bricks."

"Ns install a mental filter in our heads a little bit at a time. Before we know it, everything we do, say, or think, goes through this filter. 'Will he get upset if I do/say/think this? Will he approve/disapprove? Will he feel hurt by this?' Until we can uninstall the N-filter, our actions are controlled by N to some degree."

"The humiliation, the insults, the lies, the abuse, the character defamation and on and on and on. We may understand that they are 'sick', but then it is just us understanding them again. It doesn't really help us much to heal our pain."

"When we get to feeling too good, too happy, too satisfied, too optimistic, too excited, too anything that the N was not responsible for, then it is the N's job to rip that feeling away from us."

"Was mine a charismatic psychopath or a garden-variety N? I just don't know 100% what he is capable of. Maybe he doesn't either. It's a very good thing to be scared sometimes, especially when tempted to N-dip. It's not only our emotional wellbeing at stake here. It can be our physical (health included) safety as well."

"You may see in the man a part of yourself that is missing. A good man can help supply a feeling of wholeness and inner peace. He can help make you feel safe. An N can spot this better than anyone else. He goes after it like the drumstick at the Thanksgiving dinner. He knows people because of an over-developed inner sense. He reads people for a living. His needs are greater than yours, but he denies it to all. You may face on occasion anxiety and fear, but his is more intense and always with him. It is inevitable that the two of you will find each other. You are looking and so is he. He has the advantage because of his over-developed inner sense."

"They memorise body language and can spot a person who might feel a little vulnerable a mile away."

"My motto from here on out is: If someone or something (including me) in my life is conducting themselves in such a way that they can be seen on Jerry Springer, it's time to take out the garbage!!! When you stop taking their behaviour personally and see their antics as a true reflection on their character, it becomes absolutely nauseating."

"That's the way he conditioned you to respond. You know that bad things happen when you do something other than what he wants you to do, which may change based on his whim. Cut it, now. Cut the cord, and never look back."

"Of course, as normal human beings, we search inside ourselves for answers. That is precisely what the N never does. If he did, he would go for therapy forthwith. It is natural to wonder how we could be fooled so easily and so ruthlessly. Ever watch sleight of hand? Well, it is the same. You are fooled by the speed and skill of the 'magician' or the card sharp. But, and this is the but, it is only an illusion. Always remember that. You are healthy. The N is not. The best way to do battle with this situation is to walk away, to grind the memories under your heel, and look to better things."

"I had an N for a partner, and he built me up like yours and made me feel good, and then, straight afterwards, he brought down the hatchet and cut me out of his life. Don't be fooled - just as he opened up, so can he close up - and heaven help you when he does."

"Don't worry, he didn't pick you because you are weak or an easy target. He picked you because you have all the qualities he wants and can't have. The problem is, while he was, as we say, sucking you dry he caused you over time to feel confused, edgy, distracted and all the things you described. We loved these men and why wouldn't we? In the beginning they make us feel so special and comfortable and loved. It's later when, like you described, our minds are reeling because we know something is 'off' but can't put our fingers on it that we start searching around and find ourselves here. Then all the pieces start to fall in to place. People with NDP are master manipulators, subtle and strong at the same time. You have been brainwashed and it's going to take a while to detox but you'll be all right. It's important not to blame yourself but get on with detaching both physically and mentally. Not easy and not pleasant."

"THE FIRST GIANT RED FLAG ... needed instant gratification. It felt like he was needy. Had to spend every moment together. Pushed the sex so insistently. The relationship did not form naturally, it was rushed and he dictated the pace ... totally controlled and manipulated things in spite of all my efforts to slow it down."

"I guess there were red flags everywhere, but I had no idea what narcissism was."

"Looking back on ALL the Ns I've ever known and merged with, I see there WERE signs within minutes of meeting the N that they were grossly selfish, immoral, sex-addicted or something was definitely 'off' that I couldn't explain. I didn't honour my intuition, gut feelings and instinct. The truth is that I had almost no experience setting healthy boundaries."

"He also admitted to being 'difficult' and 'moody' - so yes, if someone says this in the early stages of a relationship, I think the red flags should definitely be up. They simply cannot sustain 'niceness' for any period of time - to anyone - unless they want something from them, or unless that person can offer them something."

"I pushed the gnawing out of my mind, relaxed and suspended judgement for a while when his behaviour or stories of his past rang as odd. I just figured I was only hearing bits and pieces and chose to wait to hear the whole story from him before I concluded anything about his personality. I should have paid more attention to my 'gut instinct'."

"NPD is serious, big-time stuff."

"Life is a superficial game for him and you are a pawn on his board. Is that what you want to be, a pawn in the hands of a madman?"

"I don't know, what nastiness your Ns did before but I can see a lot of HOOKS in your story. If your N displays off and on again behaviour BEWARE! My ex N knew how to hook me by drawing me into her sad stories. You may be your Ns main Source of Supply right now and it's true you may even know more about your N then anyone else will ever know. My N still wants to be in contact with me because I too know my x-N better than anyone else. But remember, some Ns like to be MYSTERIOUS because it keeps them in control while you're dancing to FIGURE them out."

"The N will not change, you must absolutely keep this before your mind. But the N is constantly 'paying' in his internal hell, which is the essence of his disorder. In this sense 'what goes round, comes round'."

"The N is like bog-fire (jack-o'-lantern). You race after him, and race into the marsh, where you are swallowed up and suffocated. The N will suffocate all that is good in you, will twist your psyche until you don't know who you are yourself, eventually your own face will not seem your own in the mirror. Yes, it gets that bad, believe me."

"The N is bad even for your looks - reason enough in itself to leave him quickly. He will make you feel ugly, unwanted, inadequate, not up to his standard, no matter how intelligent, good-looking, or smart you are. He makes you feel like this so that you are in line with his dreadful feelings about himself."

"I have been apart from my N almost 2 years, yet periodically he keeps coming back in my life. Not only is he narcissist, he is bipolar as well, not to mention he also has a chemical dependency problem."

"The devaluation was as shocking and devastating as it was unexpected."

"He's built up a pile of adversaries and victims over his 73 years and anyone who remembers anything about him realise the scum underneath."

"I think that is part of what they like to do to their targets. Abandon the target, leave them hanging, right in the middle of a sentence. And, you, having emotions, just have to get it out."

"I can only offer a comparison: a person who has been in a wheelchair since infancy cannot have any notion of what it feels like to walk, run, jump, do gymnastics, ride a bike etc. The person with NPD is in the same position, an emotional cripple, whose experience of life bears no resemblance to the ordinary person's."

"One thing I do have to remind myself of all the time is this. They are always looking for who they are in someone else."

"When I asked him why he had stopped terrifying me, he said: 'It didn't work'. What this says about him is that his behaviour was not out of control, as one might think because it was so bizarre, but a strategy. He stopped using that strategy when it didn't achieve his ends. That's important to remember when dealing with a true N."

"N's are notoriously bad gift-givers. My ex-N only used to give gifts to me he had received as free samples from representatives."

"Since my N told me he wanted a divorce, I have been amazed at the people who have come up to me and said they never liked the way he treated me and that I will be so much better off without him ... and I thought they liked him."

"Any apparent (and spurious) remission of NPD is just that – fake. The individual is marshalling his/her forces for the next round, which will be one hundred times worse than what went before. Believe me."

"The one you married, the terrific guy, was the False Self. When you finally realise that the horror he became, is the Real Self, then you understand NPD and you understand the nightmare for all of us."

"I rationalised and made excuses until I was blue in the face. When there was no possible excuse for certain behaviours he would come up with a sob story that I 'rationalised' and fell for. That's why I was perfect NS. I will never go there again. I am not a slave for anyone!"

"I stayed far away from him. But he would not leave me alone. I was extremely violated by this person and it took 7 years of intensive therapy to overcome the injuries I suffered because of him."

"He has never been empathetic towards anyone and has no idea how much pain he causes people when he makes choices that affect them."

"I have a very strong supportive network who keep reminding me that I am a worthwhile human being. They have told me however that the years spent with him have altered me, made me nervous and anxious and questioning my capabilities. It's insidious and you never even realise you are changing."

"He has this vindictive, mean streak in him. He knows exactly which buttons to push and can tell you to go to hell and you'll look forward to the trip."

"After about a month no contact, he was back on bended knees begging to 'negotiate his surrender' to me. He asked me to marry him. I fell for it again and the drinking started again. Shortly after the wedding, the fighting started again. I realised that drinking was lowering my inhibitions and I let out all of the anger I was still carrying from the prior devaluation. Then I discovered all his lies regarding his business, which he considered 'his little secret'. After 6 months of marriage he came home from a business trip, waited 'til the next morning after I left for work and moved out."

"Now he's suddenly devout. 'Jesus' is a verb or noun in every sentence. He carries three Bibles (a pocket-sized one for reading on the train, a medium one, and a large one for Sundays). Unreal. This same man is having an affair with a woman who is married. She is entirely dependent on him financially, and has left her husband and two sons. Her life is now becoming the wreck my life used to be. Sometimes, I too, wish I could just tell her 'Run!' but I don't dare. I just hope she believes her eyes, instead of his lies ... and saves herself."

"Don't tell them ANYTHING you aren't prepared to get shoved up your butt later ... or down your throat, or in your heart in the form of a dagger. And of course there are those things you tell them that you have to be prepared to have TWISTED into things they can shove..."

"He got hooked on the computer for NS. Totally ignored his children. Never responded to them when he came home from work. The computer took over his whole life. He was having an affair with his co-worker, at the same time having affairs with women online."

"As far as I can see clowning around with an N is like clowning around with a moray eel. In the end it's no fun. The N does not want to get close, they ONLY want ATTENTION. End of story."

"They take bad things that have happened to them and turn it into NS."

"N will have to make someone else's life miserable. It won't be mine! Better her than me! I think some Ns remarry quickly so that SHE won't have time to find out about him! She'll be in too deep before she knows it. The quicker he can get married ... the quicker he can quit playing the 'nice' game and get back to the real him!"

"<u>Sam Vaknin's book</u> and <u>this entire site</u>, has been the most helpful. Please read every cruel word that he writes. Truth is in it. These network friends will validate, listen, stay close or send you on your way-whatever you need."

"Ex-N was always insensitive about what he said to me and he always choose he words carefully as to obtain a look of shock and hurt in my face."

"I know the pain of hearing horrible, insulting remarks only to be told that it was merely a 'joke' and how I have 'no sense of humour'... I tell him that his jokes aren't funny to me, but I realise now that that's exactly what he wants to hear. I spend my days in constant anxiety because I know the next blow up is just around the corner."

"With an N, you cannot accumulate a store of MEMORIES of what you have meant to them. Your meaning is only in the here and now. This is why a husband can immediately abandon a wife who becomes crippled or has a life-threatening illness or who otherwise is no longer 'Miss step & fetch it', and who might even (HORRORS of HORRORS) NEED something from the N."

"Basically I think there are 3 categories of things Ns say:
1. Lies;
2. Projection;
3. Words to intentionally humiliate, hurt and degrade the person that loves them."

"It is not surprising then, to discover that the N has many alters, many secret lives, and they count on others to reinforce the idea that they 'would never do such a thing' and that they 'are not like that'."

"If a past girlfriend or wife dumped him, in the new location he may say that his wife recently died of cancer! This is to generate a little community sympathy for himself and opens doors for him to be accepted into the community. Then he gets busy, finding one or more targets to abuse. Stripped naked, the N is an ugly picture, without all of his/her illusions, and the fantasies dissolve."

"My N husband (who I'm finally divorcing after 18 years - 18 years in which he only got worse each year) said, on our very first date:

'You'll never do better than me'. One of many warning statements, each of which stunned me, but his persuasive charm won out. A charm that disappeared, literally, the day after we were married. Then, when he was in a towering rage after returning from a trip, I was completely perplexed at what he was angry about. When I finally asked him, he turned to me with the most malevolent glare, and said: 'YOU! You are what is wrong with me. You are what's making me angry'. But there was no action or incident related to me that he could attribute this anger to. In fact, he had been away at a trade show while I took care of our 5 young children. Nothing was ever good enough."

"Discovering that your parents have NPD is traumatising. I am an only child. I was married 6 months and my wife became pregnant. My parents accused my wife of plotting to exclude them. When she denied this, they refused to listen. Over the years they kept making more severe accusations, and never accepting my wife's answers. They babysat our 2 year-old and he woke up crabby. They started a huge fight, berating us for bringing him to their house asleep, an obvious effort to make their time with him miserable. After another incident in June, my parents threatened to end our relationship. They still blame my wife for all our problems only this time they attacked me. I told them: 'If this is what you want I will not stop you'. No contact since. I wish I would have been more blunt a lot sooner. I should have said years ago – 'Either stop making accusations and get along with my wife, or we won't see you!' The outcome would be the same but I would have saved years of frustration and stress on my marriage."

"Both of my parents are Ns. My mother is much more of a behind-the-scenes N. Her manipulations and repeated accusations have ended our relationship after 7 years of hell."

"It has ruined my entire life and my daughter's. If a doctor told her that I needed rest and no stress to recover ... she would rush over, beat on my windows and say horrible things to me ... sounds like she wants to hasten my death. It hurts. I need a mother. I am a mother and can not even grasp the concept of a mother's ability to be this cold and cruel, yet act like an angel to others. It's as if no one believes me."

"My advice – run far away before your relationship with her destroys your children. My daughter is starting to show the toll of just being witness to my mother's treatment of me. She will strike when you least expect ... she will lure you in with sweetness and tricks, and when you are feeling hopeful ... she will bring you down with one cruel perfectly-timed remark ... and you will crash in heartbreak again and again. They do not improve ... they get worse."

"She is evil to me and I have tried 51 years to have a mother and never have, never will."

"On only a few occasions did I 'stick-up for my rights' with my dad. Each time he flew into a rage. The worst was when he was out of town the day my husband and I bought a new home. When I told him on the phone about our purchase, he went stark raving mad, yelling and screaming about how stupid I was to not have waited for HIM to decide if the house was right for us. I told him it was our life and ... well the rest just wasn't pretty. As you can see the thought of any discussion about my 'feelings' with this man makes me very nervous indeed."

"He told me the psych counselour they were seeing told him and his fiancée to spend more 'quality' time together and not take his kids on the weekends he was supposed to. I called him on that one and said: 'Any counselour who recommends your wants over the needs of dependent children ought to have their license revoked'. Well, he look astonished, then started immediately back-pedalling and said: 'That's not what I meant, you misunderstood'. He never saw me or his kids for the next two months."

"A divorced father to his 8 year-old daughter during visitation weekend, upon a conflict, the father whips the daughter around by the shoulders, gets down on her level to look her square in the eyes and says angrily: 'You can come up here and see me as long as you don't interfere in my life!' This is the statement that has come back to haunt me my entire life. I have had no contact with my father since I was 21 years old. I am now 37."

"Just this last week, she asked me to stop by her work with the baby (she needs to let all the people she works with think she is a wonderful mother). When I got there, the baby was in a new outfit that I bought and dressed her in, and the N said to nobody in particular but addressing the baby: 'Who dressed you this morning? You look like a bum!' She's gets 2 birds with one stone. She devalues and degrades me and the baby all in one statement. I get the same 'Can't you take a joke' right after she insults me."

"I need to tell you that the children my N professed to love, he was abusing sexually. I stayed with him for 16 years - and he abused my elementary school age daughter for 4 years. She repressed everything. GET OUT. If he hates you, he hates your daughter and may abuse her if he hasn't already."

"I have been divorced for one year now from an N. My problem is I can't break off contact with him because we have a 5 year-old child together. After 3 years of paying very little attention to her, he became 'super dad' when I filed for divorce. How do I minimise the manipulation of my daughter? He will try anything to get my attention, including making her suffer emotionally and physically."

"He also did bad things, hoping he would get caught, and punished. This was the consistent pattern in his life and that is very sick, indeed. He justified his abandonment of all those children by saying: 'They'd be much better off without me'. He ran away, over and over."

"When I hear people who have no children talk about a narcissist or psychopath having 'parental rights' or when I hear a divorcing mom voicing guilt for depriving her child(ren) of their father, I always want to say, please, you don't know what it is like. And I want to say, please don't judge mothers and mothers don't be harsh with yourselves."

"Children will, many times in a child custody fight, choose the narcissistic parent over the non-narcissistic one. Narcissists can convince a child that they are the most desirable parent and they are also capable of convincing the child (as well as psychologists and judges) that momma does not love them, but only uses and controls them. You see, narcissists project their own pathology onto others."

"Someday Family Law specialists, Family Court judges, court appointed child advocates and psychologists who prepare reports for the courts will be educated about the personality disordered. A child's right to not be victimised should come to be seen as more important than parental 'rights'."

"I always got the feeling that my sister and I were both Dad's little scientific experiment in genetics. It wasn't so much that my parents got married and had a family as they bred kind of a 'Nazi-esque' experiment to create a little genius on my Dad's part to fulfil his expectations. My sister was the main focus of this experiment, I was the back up unit."

"A narcissist is a child, a spoiled, self-centred child. No little kid wants to have to work at caring for and entertaining another child. His payoff comes from you not wanting him to see the child. Even playing 'super dad' for someone or some group they are trying to impress can't do the job forever, or even grandparents or the people at church seldom provide enough NS every single time to make it a worthwhile expenditure of energy."

"He hated Christmas, he thought children were an expense, a noose around your neck for a life time that's why he didn't want them."

"My mother and father have always bad mouthed me to my family and all of their friends. I can't say I ever tried to 'handle' it though. The way I felt about it was that I know myself. I know them for who they really are. I have seen how low they are capable of stooping. I figured I didn't need to dignify their disgusting behaviour with any explanations to people. If they chose to believe my parents, I didn't consider them my friends. If they couldn't tell a lie or a load of horse crap when they heard it, especially considering they have known me all my life, I didn't need them in my life anyway. It was no great loss to me. I just let my parents go on ranting and raving."

"She mentioned something my father (her brother) had been saying about me. I reminded her of the real story. She was there from the beginning. She had merely forgotten the real story because, as all narcissists do, my father is really good at seeming sincere when he's changing facts to suit him, (also known as lying). She recalled vividly what I was telling her. This finally happened about 2 years ago. She was outraged at my father's lies. She straightened everyone out by telling them the truth. Now people are on to him. He has changed since then, and is more careful about how he acts towards me, and seems to have a nicer attitude around me. Of course the damage is already done."

"I have found as I am recovering from the damage my parents have done to me, thanks to Suite 101 and Sam's book. I no longer need to hold myself responsible for them or other people's happiness in any way. I have discovered a new, higher self esteem. Before, I couldn't even recognize when I didn't like someone. I would blame the discomfort I felt when I was around someone I didn't like, on

MY shyness or MY own social disorder. I thought I was such a loser that I wasn't worth another person's respect, kindness or honesty. Ns do this to people's souls. They try to kill the soul."

"My mother is very narcissistic, so I was never allowed to have my feelings and emotions if they encroached on her perfect image of herself."

Return

Oh, What a Tangled Web They Weave

Lies, Lies and More Lies

"I lie. Compulsively and needlessly. All the time. About everything. And I often contradict myself. Why do I need to do this? To make myself interesting or attractive. In other words, to secure Narcissistic Supply (attention, admiration, adulation, gossip)."

Article: Pseudologica Fantastica by Sam Vaknin
http://www.suite101.com/article.cfm/npd/63886

"They tell lies, even when there is no need to tell a lie. But telling the lie makes the game more interesting, for them, but leaves others in a state of confusion. Since they do this all the time and seldom tell the truth, that makes them pathological liars. With many years of practise, they become very convincing liars."

"They are very good at what they do and fool a lot of people, for a long time. Asking the question does not mean you will hear a truthful answer. Eventually, the truth comes out, because they get tangled up in their own webs of deceit."

"My ex-husband used to tell HUGE lies about me. Lies that always made ME look bad and HIM look like a martyr (when the opposite was true). I didn't realise this until AFTER we separated and, Boy, was it devastating! I thought that I knew ALL the horrors, to find out there were even more ... I didn't think I could take the pain!"

"An N also puts themselves into a 'zone' and their pupils dilate when they tell a lie, or they look away, to say the words."

"The lies, the flirting, the lies, the comparing, the lies, the ambivalence, the lies, the belittling, the lies, the teasing, the lies, the built up promises, the lies, the setting up for disappointment. Did I mention the lies?"

"They may spread lies about you, but in the long run, the truth will prevail. Others will figure out that what the N says, has no basis, in fact. So carry on, by moving toward something which is a lot healthier, for you. Take it as a very expensive learning experience."

"When I think back, every time he opened his mouth – another lie tripped off his tongue – but the sad thing was, he truly believed what he was saying."

"She used to lie and cheat all the time years ago. How is it that I managed to end up with another liar and cheater? My recent ex girlfriend told me recently that she can flick her feelings off and on, and that she feels empty inside. I had no idea that she would come home one day and just flick her feelings off for me... How could I have missed this one? Stunned again."

"N would lie when the truth would save his neck."

"My ex-N would look me straight in the eyes and lie his ass off. I knew he was lying, and he knew I knew he was lying, but he would do it anyway."

"Before he left, I said: 'I want my self back! I should have followed my original instinct'. He said: 'You just cancelled out the last 4 years'. I said: 'No, your lies, omissions of the truth, lack of character, integrity, responsibility, empty promises, cancelled out the last 4 years'."

"My ex-undiagnosed-female-N lied every time she opened her mouth. As time goes on, and I slowly verify some of the information, I have found that she has lied to me twice, and admitted it once. She said she was just joking (that's what a narcissistic psychopath does when caught, they just reframe it as a joke or whatever). What some of these liars do is throw a lot a truth in too, so if you check out a few things, and find it is true, then you think, well, everything is true. That's exactly what they are hoping for. For me it is hard to imagine the amount of lying that went on, the deceptions, the spin, the manipulation."

"When I would confront him about lying he would begin to laugh. He was truly evil."

"Do Ns know what they're doing when they're projecting? Probably not, but I think if it can be pointed out to them with proof, perhaps they can begin to understand the lies in their own thinking. Then we have to deal with the fact that even knowing what they're doing, and how unfair and hurtful it is to us, they may not care ... due to their lack of compassion for anyone else, and because they are emotional sadists."

Return

Reclaiming Sanity:
Understanding, Coping, Boundaries

*"'There MUST be something good and worthy under the hideous façade.'
'NO ONE can be that evil and destructive.'
'He must have meant it differently.'
This is magical thinking. Gullibility, selective blindness, malignant optimism – these are the weapons of the beast. And the abused are hard at work to provide it with its arsenal."*

Article: <u>The Malignant Optimism of the Abused</u> by Sam Vaknin
http://www.suite101.com/article.cfm/npd/68862

"Of course he wants you to believe that his reason for leaving is YOUR FAULT ... this is all part of the disorder right. Don't buy into this. Be real with yourself ... and your memories. You know deep down that you tried your best with this disordered person ... but it was a NO WIN situation. Always keep real with yourself and what you have learned about the disorder ... don't let your mind play head games with you."

"Realisation of what he really is will take time to soak in ... but you will feel better in time. Think back on a time in your life where you were completely shattered about something and thought that you would never recover ... AND YOU DID. Just as you will with this. Please reach out to us anytime ... this place, these kind, understanding people helped me every step of the way."

"When you find yourself romanticising him, read <u>Sam Vaknin's FAQs</u>. They will keep you grounded. And when you feel like venting, or raging post here!"

"Please give up trying to figure out why he says what he says ... does what he does. It's truly a pointless pursuit and it offers little comfort in the end."

"The hardest thing is saying to yourself: 'I cannot go back THERE ... so I must move forward'. Maybe it was familiarity that kept us there ... but fear is my biggest hang-up. Fear of the unknown! I guess we traded a few moments of happiness with them when actually it was hell on earth!"

"She actually never had emotions for me nor does she harbour guilt over what she's done. I mean, I just can't fathom that. She said so many beautiful things to me! The reality that all that may have been a crock, is overwhelmingly inconceivable."

"It's hard not to think what they're doing now and who they're doing it with. I have to stop myself and remind myself if I were with him right now he would be making me clinch with some nasty negative remark or subtly insulting me or something that made my gut draw up!"

"When I'm tempted to respond to him, as I am now, I read here and post here. It's a good reality check. We can so easily forget the harm they do."

"It was then I realised I was still hanging on ... like I was addicted to the N. I want to be free and away from it all. I want my mind to be free of the N infection."

"This reconciliation between the N and myself was short-lived. His true colours emerged, once again. But being able to document my every-day experience with him helped me to make the final decision to move on. I know that I'm far from recovering, and who knows I may make that mistake by N-dipping one more time, but if my experiences serve to help anyone else on this board, then I feel like I have at least accomplished something."

"I'm learning to take things one day at a time. If I N-dip, I just get back up, dust myself off and try again."

"I wanted to talk to ex-N so much today. Yet the desire to N-dip made me very anxious. It's as though my need for him, for someone so very bad for me, is finally becoming ego-dystonic. The urge to be with him creates strong inner dissonance because I know if I contact him it's emotional suicide. Still, I am in so much pain. I can hardly work. My job seems overwhelming."

"People on the site call it 'N-dipping'. It is like fighting an addiction. So, if you are tempted to slide, it's entirely understandable. At one time you felt great love and passion for this man, and there is some part of you that WISHES he wasn't what you know him to be, WISHES it wasn't all true, that it didn't happen the way it did, and that you could GET BACK that guy you thought he was. I was always tempted to think maybe this is some sort of aberration, something going on in his life, stress, mental illness, and that the OTHER GUY, the one I fell in love with was the REAL HIM. I hated having to finally face the fact that I fell in love with a Jekyll and Hyde facade. It absolutely sucks."

"N-dipping is not sinful it just doesn't go anywhere ... except as NS. It is also very painful to let go of all the hopes and dreams. I'm glad you have reached out here ... as support is absolutely a necessary part of your (and our) recovery."

"For what it's worth, I did my N-dipping BEFORE I even knew what NPD was. I had a death wish for many years because I was in so much emotional pain. I lived like that for about 20 years. I got to the point where I could hardly function at all. Everything I did, was by rote. Now that I have the information about NPD, it is much easier to stay away from my N husband, emotionally. I still have times when I get depressed and unsure about everything, but those times are less and less."

"They just don't change and the games become more cruel. The devaluation becomes worse and more painful every time we go back. That's why I think some people think N-dipping is healing in a way, because you see the patterns repeating themselves. It won't be too long before you are able to detach from him emotionally and one day you will look at his antics and thank God you are no longer one of his victims."

"You can be certain that the winner in the end will be you, with your mind and soul intact. You have pinpointed the heart of the matter. You can love, will always be able to love. He can't, and never will. He is an emotional cripple who cannot even love himself. You will move forward in life, but he will remain, always, in the shadow-lands of his disorder."

"Then you get to the point where you could give a rat's ass about what other people think about you, because you know you're fine, just fine!"

"I am so lucky that I have absolutely no sentiment towards my ex-N left. The only emotion I have is fear and justifiably so."

"My pain over ex-N has been replaced with disdain. I hope this feeling hangs on. I never thought it would even come. After 30 years of being together, I thought that was all there was for me. Life is so much better now. All I needed was a little distance so I could get some perspective."

"The thing with us is we see good in other people and dismiss the bad. Like you I always go out of my way to help people and I get used ... 'sucker' on my forehead is a good way of saying it. I am a magnet for these people."

"I don't mind feeling depressed, I know this is somehow necessary before the healing. But it feels like my life is going up and down from day to day. I feel so helpless in the a.m. and so determined hours later only to feel exhausted by the next day."

"No one ever builds true happiness at the expense of someone else."

"It's a multi-layered illness to be in a relationship with an N. In recovery the first detachment is letting go of the N and the next is letting go of one's mirage-like illusions about the N, and the next is healing one's own relationship with one's True Self, and the next is learning to connect in a healthy way with others who can share a MUTUAL relationship..."

"It is difficult and sad for mothers to deal with a non-loving child, whether the child has a personality disorder or not. But if they are NPD and we find out more about this disorder, it is natural to wonder, 'What part did I play in this?'"

"I was sitting here wondering why I can't mentally rid myself of my own creep. He's not even a part of my life anymore. I don't see him, hear from him, talk or communicate with him ... but he's inside my head and driving me crazy. He goes everywhere with me. He's a leech, a soul-sucker. I want rid of his presence, rid of his power, rid of his control over my mind. But yet I let him hang on inside my head sapping at the good person I used to be."

"I'm alone, but not lonely. I'm not elated, but I'm not sad – I'm not mad but I am disappointed ... but it's my time to learn, we never learn anything when the road is smooth. We learn survival when we are taxed, and the road is lumpy. RIGHT?"

"Extreme highs and lows (which is what life in the shadow of the N is about) are not healthy. Such extremes are exhausting, as you second-guess what is going to be the next high or low. And, the lows sure do get lower, and the rages increase, and the devaluation sets in like a rot."

"As per the men, I don't get close to them as of yet, even though I crave the affection I lacked for four years. I would like to be touched and loved but even thinking about doing such with a normal man seems unreal. I think to myself 'what if I can't enjoy his closeness?' and 'what if I won't feel anything?' These are the thoughts I have."

"At the time I thought I'd never be strong again, but in retrospect I would have to say it as better to have loved and LEARNED than to have not loved at all. Because now I know, beyond a shadow of a doubt, that I will never allow anyone to treat me that way again."

"Remember, no matter what's going on in your life, it's YOUR responsibility to choose how you will respond. It doesn't mean you won't hurt or be angry. It doesn't mean you should ignore what you're feeling either. Not being a victim and taking responsibility means feel the pain, acknowledge the shock, be mad, pissed off, etc., while looking for the LESSON. Keep on going in a way that honours you and who you really are."

"And, of course, after all the words from him telling me how much he didn't want me around any more, how he needed a change etc., he wouldn't leave or start the proceedings. I had to do all that. Part of his illogical 'rules'. Mostly, I don't believe he thought I would ever go."

"Leaving finally took every bit of strength I had left, especially when I find myself with very little money and starting a career at a time when I should be having the time of my life. I looked forward to this part of my life for a long time! Silly of me. I really should have known better."

"If more people had 1/100 the compassion, insight, and decency of people on this board (or if Ns had 1/100 the compassion, insight, and decency of most people), this world would be so much better."

"Trying to apply normal human qualities to an N is impossible. He's like a 5 year-old who got a new toy. Does he care anything about the old one? Of course not. You not only have the hurt of getting dumped by the N, but the realisation that he is an N. That's a double whammy in anybody's book."

"If you were given a textbook on Ns and told to study them, with no knowledge of the actual person you would have one heck of a time trying to figure them out. Getting stung by one and then trying to figure yourself and them out too is where we're all at here. Go ahead, cry anywhere, anytime. I could hug you because you have normal emotions."

"I've lived with mine for 37 years. I'm in the process of breaking away and getting a divorce. But, believe me, he has done serious emotional damage to me. I too, am in therapy and currently exploring the Post-Traumatic Stress Disorder concerning myself. You ended up staying in this mess because you thought that somehow you could make it better ... but there is no better. When we finally come to THAT realisation is when we start picking up the pieces of ourselves to get on with life."

"Reading Sam Vaknin's FAQs is like a roadmap of my experiences with N parents. It serves as constant reminders to us that the Ns have the problem!"

"...in every tear is a seed of healing."

"Today I did two things for myself. The first was to have lunch with a girlfriend. It was very uplifting. I kept thinking that I was glad I was no longer with N. The second was to spend two hours out at the river. It was wonderful."

"He was like a ball and chain around my neck. All Ns are. Every day I pray to God to give me strength and help me deal with this. The key is, I don't want it anymore. I really don't. I don't want to be with someone who doesn't truly care for me and love me the way I want and deserve to be. I'm so tired of thinking of him and his supposed emotional barriers and childhood traumas. Yes it's sad, but I shouldn't suffer because of it."

"Many years ago, a marriage counselour told me that you simply cannot give to others if you aren't getting something back yourself. Those who give you positive feedback help, I know, but they can't be enough. Part of the reason your depression is so severe is that you are giving away more than you are receiving in return. You need to correct that. You need to be sensitive to draining situations and draining people, then you have to avoid them. Yes, you will feel guilty at first, but you will learn to be able see things in ways that are friendlier and more supportive of yourself."

"Remember most people in this world are here to help each other. But you must first come back to this world for others to help you. Just throw yourself out to the real world and leave the narcissist behind. People will catch you and help you. First you have to know that people in this world are not here to get you – they are with you. You must first help yourself back to this world, to the point where others can start helping you. Remember: 'A loving heart is the truest wisdom.'"

"Some days will seem OK, then others you'll feel lower than low. That's to be expected. Just remember that he's the defective one, not you. It's difficult to digest that a person can be so mean and shallow on the inside when they can 'appear' to be so wonderful on the outside. You're not alone, and you're definitely not to blame for his behaviour. He'll do it to everybody who crosses his path."

"The learning from experience part of life is the hardest, but I believe it means the most. You have learned that people like him don't change themselves inside, just the scenery outside. Very shallow existence indeed."

"It is not unusual to have anxiety and panic attacks in the wake of the N-experience. It is in fact, quite normal, and they can last for many months afterwards."

"Final closure for me is the fact that HE IS WHAT HE IS. The carousel continues to turn for the N but not for me ... any longer."

"Another thing that helped me through the post N experience, which I still feel I'm in just further along the path, is to REMEMBER it's the beautiful, wonderful, lovely, top-notch qualities about you that attracted him in the first place."

"Every time I go into this obsessive mess I remind myself of a quote I recently read: 'You know it is real love when a person touches your life in a way (better) that you want to be a better person, and your life will never be the same after they touched yours'. They leave a mark of goodness, kindness, gentleness... (the fruits of the spirit). Does any N do that? NO!!! They touch our lives, but it's with such destruction and torture ... it was never love! I believe their mental torture is knowing they had a good person and blew it! Therefore, they move on for new supply. Let it go! It is now someone else's pain and suffering. You deserve better!"

"We need to recognise that we must CELEBRATE our increasing feistiness, our stiffer backbone, our thicker skin, our stronger boundaries, and our ability to lay aside, with lessening amounts of distress and guilt, the desire to fix, to 'be there', for yet another wounded soul. When we understand what healing is all about, when we understand that healing ourselves is the only way to attract healthy personalities, when we understand that healing ourselves is the only way to become attracted to healthy personalities, then we will heal."

"Can I urge those of you still in the throes of the immediate aftermath of the N experience to care for yourselves physically, to try (yes, I know it is so very, very hard) not to 'introspect' too much, and to reach out to others. You will be surprised at the degree of help available in unexpected quarters. Do something peculiar, different, totally out of character, in the line of a pursuit or hobby. The concentration required will fill your mind, and any device is valid that will take your mind off what has happened."

"I believe it is possible to forgive, genuinely forgive in one's heart and soul, and yet not put oneself in danger or refuse to hold someone accountable for their actions."

"You know in your heart and that ache in your gut! You just dread taking that step. And yes, he will try to charm you again until he knows he's lost and he'll move on."

"I have learned lots of stuff about myself that I never before had to bother looking at. There IS a reason you are so attached and fell hard for this type. Finding that reason doesn't make the sorrow completely go away, but it does help to make sense of things."

"N boyfriend to distraught girlfriend over his emotional and physical withdrawal: 'You could have everything you wanted if you would just...' The ending always changes arbitrarily so as the girlfriend could never get it right to 'get what she wanted' which was physical and emotional closeness."

"I still get stuck wanting what I can't have, a healthy, loving, honest, open relationship with a person who only mimicked these things and then left me holding the bag."

"I can only say to those with doubts, with ideas of 'fixing it' - just don't. Move away and try to cut your losses. Why sit down to the table again to be dealt another bum hand?"

"Then, fool that I was, tried to become a crusading Pollyanna, armed with books, clinical data, case histories - I valiantly tried to cure him. Sam Vaknin calls it magical thinking and he's so right. I gave up. It's useless and a total waste of my time when I needed to concentrate on getting me better and getting on with my life."

"I have been with my N for 11 years and was completely disillusioned by him. I did everything I could to make things work and tried fixing the unfixable. He exploited me and other women for years. I'm done with him and have decided that I'm going to move forward with my life."

"If I absolutely WANT to stop the N, I have hundreds of ways, but if I, in the back of my head, continue playing his game, it means that I'm still denying his disease and still trying to control or heal it... I thought of the 3 'C's: I don't Cause it, I can't Control it and I can't Cure it..."

"I don't want to accept that the N can NOT do anything about himself. Our society stinks because of the 'not take responsibility for your actions' mentality. He has admitted knowing he needs help but doesn't WANT to do anything about it."

"To anyone feeling emotional and vulnerable and self-reflective ... call a close friend. Visit a loved one you haven't seen in years. Write heart-felt letters to anyone who means anything to you ... but don't give in and show remorse or regret over a narcissist. You'll only leave the encounter still hurting and they'll have their NS-fix for the week."

"One of the signs of the abuse inflicted on you is having fleeting murderous violent horrible thoughts. You are not losing your mind, it is just your natural self-preservation instinct because you are feeling so intensely trapped. You are mentally 'fighting back'. You know deep down inside you are incapable of really doing anything. But the thoughts can be frightening, especially if you have never had them before. A lot of it has to do with the fact that you are so angry that this person has you in such a position."

"I was with my husband for ten years and was completely and utterly devoted to him. Brainwashed, totally. He was my guide, my life and he almost destroyed me. Now when I think of him I feel absolutely nothing, zero. No hate, no pity, not an ounce of love - just nothing. And it's wonderful."

"I felt that emptiness also when I confronted him with the truth of him being personality disordered. Then all you think is ... how could I have been so fooled? Self-reflection is not an easy thing to do. You then have to face all aspects of yourself, shadow and light. Being able to do this is what makes us different."

"I am a firm believer that most women who accept a bad relationship had no voice as a child and suffered emotional and sometimes physical abuse. I know I did."

"Both of my sons eventually saw their N-dad for what he truly is. I didn't have to tell them or talk to them about their Dad. They figured it out. Now we (my sons and I) are very close and have wonderful times when we are together. N-Dad's name isn't even mentioned between us anymore."

"I guess I'm just feeling sorry for myself. It's been over a year since this N abandonment-nightmare began and I can't believe I still feel so bad."

"When the 'devaluation' phase began I was totally confused having been in denial for so long about the one-dimensional aspect of our relationship."

"Denial is the way we handle what we cannot handle."

"Is it like your emotions are going up and down like a roller coaster? One minute you miss him so bad you can hardly stand it, the next moment you are furious at him for never loving you the way you loved him."

"In retrospect I see how boring, predictable and exasperating living with the N was. Moody, moody, moody. It was like having an infant. My nine-year-old son was better able to control himself!"

"I am in the process of moving on with my life ... enrolled in college and also looking forward to a divorce and the day I will be REALLY free. I didn't come to these decisions easily ... I suffered for over 35 years of marriage. The greatest revelation to me has been that my marriage has been a 'figment of MY imagination'. Please don't think that he will ever change. They can't. What they are is their survival mechanism. If it wasn't for the information that I learned here I would probably be looking for a pine box! As I have taken my 'baby steps' in recovery, I find that I have regained my self-esteem. I have realised that I did everything I could to make the marriage work and when it failed, I was not to blame. I am a worthwhile person and so are you. You have suffered enough. PLEASE move on with your life! There is just so much more than life with a self-centred, ego-maniac who cares nothing for anyone except how they can serve them. Stay here and get strong. The fine people who post here have been through it all."

"You will never unlearn what you now know about narcissism. If you go back to the N, you will look at him – and you will know, and this knowledge will come between you."

"I just CAN'T believe that our relationship amounted to nothing to him. I just can't believe it! I can't even begin to understand the mind of someone like him. How could he do this?"

"I'd love to be able to pick up the phone and call him and scream and yell and cry for all of the heartache I went through (and still go through) for him... But I, like you, know that it wouldn't do any good. It's truly heartbreaking to know that someone you loved more than life itself has no way of understanding what it feels like."

"We are de-programming ourselves (at least I hope we are!) and it can only get better. When WE look in the mirror we know who is looking back at us. What does the N see when he looks for the millionth time in his mirror. Best not to dwell too much on what he sees."

"I want love and I daresay the entire human race does too. But love comes to you, and it will, maybe in the form you least expect. But it cannot be chased after and brought down with a left and a right like a bird. You cannot capture love, by its very nature. It should be a healthy interaction between two people (and you know this), not a co-dependency. So, yes, there are the fireworks, and the coloured lights, and the exhilaration, and the dangerous delight of the first days with the N. We have all experienced that, and look where it got us. Love, for me at any rate, is the person who is always there for you, and you for them, even when you are tired, down, fatigued from work, maybe not looking your best, in bed with 'flu and looking a freak. Love is, whether we like it or not, the good, old-fashioned daily slog and all it entails. Anything else is movie stuff, and a recipe for disaster."

"I hate that word co-dependent. Seems like every nice, decent person I even knew is somehow called a co-dependent."

"Take lots of care. Look in other directions. Take your mind to a quiet place. Do something you never did before."

"Don't let your mind be invaded, even by your own negative thoughts/memories, or even by what you might consider memories of the 'good' times. 'Good times' do not exist in N-land."

"To him, trust was just about sex and fidelity and had nothing to do with emotional intimacy. If you push for intimacy with an N, there is no choice for them other than to flee or devalue. There is no love there ... they don't know what it means. That's why, I liken it to talking to an alien ... they just don't get it."

"Staying with an N, or making contact with an ex-N, is like putting your hands directly on a hot stovetop to warm them. It will 'work' for five seconds before it scalds you."

"It's amazing the little details I keep remembering, and how angry they make me ... and ultimately how stupid I feel for putting up with it."

"That feeling of not getting it all out with her will fade, and you'll be glad you didn't get it all out with her, because she'd just use the information to somehow abuse you even more either now or in the future."

"Our biggest wish is that someone would be able to find a cure for NPD because it just breaks our hearts to see our partners/friends/husbands/wives with NPD suffer and inflict suffering on the people who love them most. We have no choice but to leave for our own self-preservation."

"I have separated myself from him in every way, but he persists in calling, writing, driving by, e-mailing, sending friends to communicate, etc. I want it to stop sooooo... badly but the nightmare continues."

"Of course, he didn't have a clue what I meant. Explaining the notion (that the issues I had with him were all about a lack of emotional intimacy) was just an opportunity to engage in the blame (me) game, word-salad game, pathologise (me) game, spin reality game and lure and slam game, rationalise it all away game, etc. ... in other words, I had my first brush with the devaluation cycle. Very painful and bewildering."

"Once you are crystal clear in your perception of the Ns true personality, you lose respect for them. Then you can put up with a lot, because you no longer feel the need to take what they say with any seriousness."

"Funny: Sex was not a problem, except if she didn't get enough ... and trust me it was never enough."

"You're not crazy. No way. Your anger is your weapon right now. You need to be angry. You have a right to be angry."

"Happiness is the best revenge, because that's something we're capable of but they're not. Get angry, feel the hurt, but please don't act out on revenge. Then you'd just have to feel your own shame for living outside of your own values."

"After sinking into a pit of despair, going into shock one night and shaking so bad I could not stop that shaking, I literally could not stop it. It frightened me. Then, I became angry, I get my strength from anger. The angrier I get, the stronger I get. Here I was driven into mind-numbing terror, pain, confusion. The anger became an almost welcome relief from the pain. How could he treat me that way? I had done nothing but work for our marriage. I was dumped like a bag of trash."

"Maybe it's just good, old-fashioned aversion to pain. None of us like to be hurt, and when we perceive things or situations as hurtful, we tend to avoid them. I used to avoid things too, as a reaction to all the pain I had suffered as a child. Some things should be avoided, and others should be worked through, and the trick for me has been partly learning how to tell the difference."

"What helped me was learning that I don't have to be all things to all people, and learning that I can be myself, and that is good enough for most people."

"I needed real human contact so badly after my experience with my ex-N. I enjoyed such simple things in life as to sit and have a give-and-take conversation, mutual respect, a smile, a touch. All of this without what the narcissist overlays upon social interaction. I was awed by how nice people are, how understanding, and at the same time, many, truly don't understand, yet they were human, and MAN WAS IT GOOD TO SPEND SOME TIME WITH A HUMAN!!!"

"You know that old saying that the opposite of love isn't hate, it is indifference. And, sweet woman, you are much bigger and better than he is. Don't stoop down to his level."

"Once you've had some time with zero contact with him you will see how your thinking clears and changes. Read everything here as it really helps and please keep sharing here. You'll find lots of support and comfort. When you are tempted to call him sit down here and read or write until it passes. Vent, vent, vent!"

"Why don't we go? For any combination of reasons. Take a look at the 'you' before or at the time you started going out with the N – and the 'you' later on. Never was anyone less equipped to get out by that stage – your self worth is in the gutter, you feel a failure, a deep sense of being a nothing – the things the N said to you, the insidious drip-feed of negatives, their behaviour that says so much about how little they respect or care for you. Then of course we really do have to face some of the nastiest – the what ifs, the depression, the self-hatred (how COULD I have put up with this, how DARE he did this to me without a blink of the eye – what must he have thought of me knowing I allowed him to do these things), the loneliness, sense of failure."

"My ex-N did mood swings on me too. That is, if we were going someplace, he would be fine until in the car. Suddenly, he would be down and out. When I became familiar about N disorder, I would straight up say: 'Hey you think I am going to follow in to YOUR mood you are WRONG! I'm staying happy so there you go big fellow!' Meaning: grow-up. Yea, they do that stuff. It is the other person who has the choice to NOT fall prey to the mood especially if it is a negative mood. Remember, they say the opposite of what is happening. Saying you were playing mind games 'meant' HE WAS!"

"It was only when I finally – after about 3 months – came across Sam Vaknin's site on Suite 101, that I sat in front of the screen, with a dropped jaw, poking a finger at the screen and shouting: 'That's IT – that's it – HIM!'"

"My N just casually said one day: 'Sorry if I seem a bit narcissistic' ... I ran for the computer and found this site. I began reading stories of people just like me. Everything became clear. Up until that point I was going downhill fast. I think I could 'maybe' recognise it quicker now, but you know what they say about being blinded by love ... it's true."

"As I was reading the information by Sam Vaknin, I just started crying both out of relief and frustration."

"It is here that I really talked about it. This place has been a solace for me for almost 1 year. I have told no one of this place. It is my little secret place with secret friends that I come to and talk about the hell I have been through ... and hopefully help others who are in this hell."

"I stopped contact with the N. I felt stronger again, but very lonely. I posted here often at all times of the day and night, and always received love and support."

"I can come up here onto the forum and share the 'laughing on the outside, crying on the inside' syndrome, and not get judged for feeling like this, which keeps me going. One day, I will laugh on the inside as well – and I'll have all of you, and the fun and tears we share, to thank for that. You are my lifelines. Thanks."

"Discovering [Sam Vaknin's website](#) couldn't have come at a better time! I sit here in a stupor having left my narcissist 19 days ago, and I cannot begin to describe these feelings – rage, betrayal, pain, denial, longing, emptiness, angst, jealousy – I'm all over the place with this thing. I feel like the victim of a very mean practical joke."

"The support I have received from everyone here has been what made me turn the corner away from my ex-N. I am amazed at how people who were strangers to me two months ago, and who I would not recognise on the street, have helped me walk through the worst part of it unscathed."

"But as much as we are responsible for our own life we are responsible for society around us."

"Are you willing to draw the line now and say 'no more'? If so, then you have my support and probably the support of everyone else."

"Learn as much as you can as fast as you can, protect yourself financially and emotionally."

"Do not let him get the impression that these calls are rattling you. Be brusque and impolite (nothing else will have any effect) next time he tries this."

"There are worse things than being lonely. (Living with a N)"

"I really just need to tell him once and for all: 'I am not interested in speaking with you. My personal life is my business. Please stop calling me.' Say it in an unemotional, matter-of-fact voice. Then

STOP talking to him. If he manages to get you on the phone, hang up the INSTANT you realise it's him. He will call and call, but eventually will give up and go away."

"Ask him: 'Hey, who stepped on you today?' You might get him talking about what is really bugging him rather than taking things out on you."

"Before I cut my losses and left my husband I tried valiantly to predict what he would do or say, and speak accordingly. But it didn't matter, whatever I did he would twist it to his own advantage. I agree with what you say about simple, strict language with the N. It seems the best route is as few words as possible with clear meaning. Similar to dealing with a toddler."

"My Ns love to try verbal manipulation. They're very good at it and most people fall for it time and again. It takes Ns 20-40 minutes of running the gamut of all their whining, complaining, argumentative and other persuasive tactics. Then in the end they hit my 'NO' brick-wall they have no where left to go. It's a horrible way to live but sometimes it's not possible to get them out of your life in one swift stroke so boundaries become essential survival techniques for non-Ns."

"You have a remedy in the courts: it's called PAS, Parental Alienation Syndrome. I believe that Ns practice alienating their victims from each other all the time – it's one of their mainstays. You can prove this and your child can help; when your child understands that your ex has purposely been trying to stop her from loving you – it will free her too. Fortunately, Ns are verbal and document their own crazy antics through e-mail, regular mail, answering machine messages, and their own court papers, your ability to prove PAS won't be difficult; you can use the N's own words against him. Getting counselling for yourself and your child also proves the point; that your ex is causing intentional emotional damage to you and your child. File a PAS lawsuit. That ought to scare the heck out of him and get him off your back. In the meantime keep collecting evidence – his own words and mean-spirited actions."

"Ns love spreading lies and rumours. That's one of the things they do best. When you hear about them, put up your hand, palm outward (the stop-sign position). Tell whoever it is firmly and with a chuckle 'I don't want to hear anything about N'."

"Please do help yourself set some firm boundaries. One thing that helps me is to ask myself 'would I want someone to treat my daughter this way?' More often than not the answer is 'No'. If it's not good enough for her, then it's not good enough for her mother."

"Call him on it. 'No, that's what YOU do, not me.' I've read suggestions that a victim should accuse the N of outrageous things too, it really throws them. And when they rage at you, rage back! They are counting on you NOT doing this. They are counting on you remaining a doormat, they hope you'll keep trying to be understanding, etc., so they can keep wiping their feet on you."

"Circle those dates on your calendar and make plans that can't be changed. Get tickets to a show or concert, commit to help out a friend or organisation. Edge him out. Remember, the worst thing you can do to N is ignore him or discount his importance. You are over him, you can even give him a Mona Lisa smile and keep walking."

"Using very simple assertiveness statements works with these folks, however don't expect them to like it. Trying to enlist their co-operation is useless. Only by having very firm boundaries, telling them what your decisions are, and never, ever explaining or defending yourself are you able to maintain any sanity."

"He raged, he yelled, he pouted. I went about my merry way with a slight smile on my face. The more he reacted, the more I kept calm. Now he is bending over backwards to please me. I just keep on smiling and going about my merry way."

"Why not just act uninterested and give him a flat out 'NO' with ABSOLUTELY NO EXPLANATIONS?"

"Indifference is absolutely your best tool in dealing with the N. They HATE indifference. Do not react in any way to anything he says or does. Any reaction, good or bad is supply for them. Any response you get will not be real, merely another attempt at manipulating the situation. Do not let him do that. It's what he wants. Somewhere to place the blame, and to make you feel as bad as possible. He is not 'expecting' any particular reaction. ANY reaction will do for him."

"You are going to have to be stronger than you've ever been to block him ... block e-mails, get caller ID. For your mental health and safety you have to do this to get rid of him. He will not give up easily but you know you can't afford to have him in your life. You don't owe him any explanations or even advice about NPD. His denials and excuses will only confuse you more. And you can't help him."

"After the worst of it was over, what I found to be key was to have no contact with him. None. Do not say go to hell. Do not say I love you. Do not, above all, try to sit down and have a dialogue, to reason with him. No response of any kind is the answer."

"Please, please do whatever it takes to avoid the phone. With narcissism, I suggest procrastination. Tell yourself you'll wait until tomorrow ... then tomorrow repeat that same phrase ... meaning that you never initiate contact. Put off until 'tomorrow', what you MUST NOT DO TODAY!"

"DON'T ANSWER HIS MESSAGES...
　DON'T MAKE CONTACT...
　DON'T WASTE YOUR PRECIOUS TIME...
　DON'T TOY WITH YOUR FRAGILE EMOTIONS...
　No matter how much we want to believe they're not seedy weasels...
　WE KNOW THEY ARE! And you know HE is..."

"The boundaries I found most successful are where I don't answer his 'statements presented as questions'. Never fall for his 'yes/no' response type of questions. Never ask an N a question, it's just inviting lies. Never answer a question, either, always respond 'I'll have to think about that' to give yourself time to think about what he's really trying. Whenever he asks his beating-around-the-bush questions I use the tactics of salesmen and just repeat his last 3-4 words back to him, posed as a question. When I don't want him bugging me any more I'll say: 'This is becoming annoying N'. With any luck you'll have him walking on eggshells."

"Be fully self-reliant and responsible so you never, ever have to ask him for anything. When you do say NO, the ABSOLUTE WORST thing you can do is to change your mind. Practice, practice, practice your boundary statement until you can pull it off without batting an eye. Oh, and try chuckling at his words. The humiliation alone can often cause them to disappear like a vampire at sunrise."

"I said No effectively. All I got was the infamous N rage every time I put my foot down. It is no way to live. You cannot reason with the N because they refuse to have any type of normal conversation. A relationship is supposed to be a reasonably fluid journey, not a situation where you are in 'shields up' mode all the time, and where you have to become the manipulative one. Not healthy at all. The only possible N relationship is NO N-relationship. Despite having no financial security, not even a roof of my own, I could not live in that marriage."

"If she sets up a situation where you can't walk away just give polite agreeable responses. 'Well, it's a good thing my little Suzy became a brain surgeon, or you wouldn't have become a brain surgeon.' 'Well, Aunt Mouthie, Suzy is quite a leader. Will you excuse me please?' Walk away and smile like the cat that just ate the canary. Not catty, just cool. 'My little Suzy got first place in the beauty contest, you came in second.' 'Aunt Mouthie, no one can compete with Suzy's beauty and brains. She is lovely. Excuse me, I'll be back in a bit.' Smile, walk away and don't be back. Be classy, be cautious, be secure. Take care and keep your chin up."

"Start documenting everything now! Save copies of his e-mails or copies of the Web sites that he frequents. Document how he treats your children. You can't be too detailed. It may be a pain to do but you will be glad you did. Do you work? If you leave do you have a way to support your kids on your own? I think a broken home is much better than exposing your kids to an out-of-control freak. One tip which I wish I had known when I separated from my ex-N is make him think it is all his idea. As far as the kids, you don't want him to use them as a weapon against you. Make visitations sound as though they help you out tremendously. That way he won't want contact with them. I feel for you. I've been split from my ex-N for two years and still have to deal with his control issues because of our child. I wish I didn't have to deal with him at all."

"Now this next is a rather difficult thing for some women to do, but IF you can ACT as though his exercising his visitation rights is YOUR TICKET TO FREEDOM, then this will be one of your most powerful weapons. When he shows up to pick up your daughter, be all dolled up, hair all pretty, FULL MAKEUP, 'going out' clothes and PERFUME. ACT as though you are ready to go out partying. Even check your watch if he tries to keep you even an extra second at the door. Now, if you REALLY go out (and why waste good perfume), that is all the better. This is a good time to practice being good to yourself by spending time with girlfriends, learning to line dance, taking a class, visiting a museum or art gallery, attending a movie, concert or play – or whatever. You want him to BELIEVE that his 'services' are much desired so that YOU can have SPECIAL TIME for yourself. UNPAID BABY SITTER."

"Instead of seeing yourself as one person, dealing with an unreasonable crazy person, imagine that all of us are standing right behind you, forming a group. Take strength from us, for as long as you need that, until you can fly with the eagles – on your own."

"If you want to end a relationship with a N, the formula is very simple: The narcissist analyses (and internalises) everything in terms of blame and guilt, superiority and inferiority, gain (victory) and loss (defeat) and the resulting matrix of Narcissistic Supply.

Shift the blame to yourself (I don't know what happened to me, I've changed, it's my fault, I'm to blame for this, you're constant, reliable and consistent...).

Tell him you feel guilty (excruciatingly so, in great and picturesque detail).

Tell him how superior he is and how inferior you feel.

Make this separation your loss and his absolute, unmitigated gain.

Convince him that he is likely to gain more supply from others (future women?) than he ever did or will from you.

BUT, make clear that your decision – though evidently 'erroneous' and 'pathological' – is FINAL, irrevocable and that all contact is to be severed henceforth.

And never leave ANYTHING in writing behind you."

"The best advice I've gotten here is to seem neutral as much as possible. Another tactic I've found successful is to capitalise on their laziness and irresponsibility (responsibility is too much work). My N missed a court hearing because he was simply too lazy to keep track of the date. Good documentation helps here, because they never keep track of dates, incidents, etc."

"What you can do is clearly document the things that you have done and said that you are concerned he will twist, so that you will be prepared with reasonable and truthful explanations for those things, if it ever comes to the point at which you need to defend your actions. If there is anything that you can document that will verifiably (on paper), demonstrate that the N has lied or has distorted the truth to fortify his position, find it and make sure that your attorney knows about it."

"Dealing with these people in a legal situation is very upsetting and frustrating. You have to assume that anything you say will be examined and re-examined to determine if there is any possible potential for it to be used against you. In my own situation I have shut down all avenues of communication with the N. The ONLY communication I will permit is through our attorneys. It is very frustrating to not be able to work things out and reason like normal people, but they just aren't normal. They make things up. They spew venom. They infect everyone within their sphere of influence. They truly believe that they are right and entitled to operate outside the law, and they will attempt to build a convincing case for this out of absolutely nothing. The sheer 'magic' of their ability to do this is mind-boggling in itself."

"I have the dog, the alarm system, the caller ID, 2 police reports filed, the motion detector light on 2 sides of the house, changed e-mail addresses, changed phone numbers, asked his friends to co-operate with my requests to distance myself, returned all his priority mail to sender, but I haven't yet done what you suggested regarding forwarding his e-mails. I'll try that. I've avoided that mainly because of the hurt that it might cause others. I think that the only way for me to make this nightmare stop is to 'shine a brighter light' on the darkness that he creates. I have also returned everything that was his. I have tried to literally and figuratively erase all the symbols and remembrances of the pain and agony that he brought into my life and the lives of anyone close to me. I do not want to ever forget the very excruciating lessons that I hope I have ingrained in my brain through this experience. If the pain needs to stay with me for the rest of my life as a reminder of what was, then so be it."

"There is only one way for you (and the rest of us) to go - and that is onwards, upwards and away."

"I know from past experience that there does come a day when you can look back and laugh at some of this stuff. So my wish is that everyone here has a moment like that today."

"The figures seem to indicate that a minimum of 1% (probably 3% and perhaps up to 5%) of the population above the age of 10 are narcissists. Now, factor in the parents, spouses, colleagues, friends, children, the children's families... This is the biggest under-diagnosed mental health pathology ever. Many researchers

also believe that all Cluster B personality disorders (Histrionic, Antisocial, and Borderline) have an underlying foundation of pathological narcissism. This is getting close to 10% of the adult population. Staggering numbers."

Excerpts from the Archives of the Narcissism List - Part 1
http://samvak.tripod.com/archive1.html

Return

On the Funny Side of the Street

...(Our Blunders, Bloopers, Typos, One-Liners and Jokes)

Cyber abbreviations:
ROFL = rolling on the floor laughing,
LOL = laughing out loud

"For me, it finally became such a chore to always look my best, walk just right, talk just right ... in short to be perfect. It just isn't happening. I'm sorry, but I'm not June Cleaver ... I don't vacuum in a dress & heels!! LOL"

"One morning I asked if he'd like a cup of coffee to drink on the way to work. His response: 'I don't understand. Some days you prepare the coffee, and other days you ask if I want coffee. There is no consistency, I don't know what to expect.' Jeez Louise, it's coffee, not sex!!!"

"Anybody bringing a bullwhip? I'm going to need some self-punishment."

"By the way it won't take long before you reelize I don't spell check ot profread.
   ...and I no longer korrect you! LOL"

"Gee, I'm glad you fessed up on the spell checking... I was starting to think you had been spending too much time at Walmart! LOL
   ...yue leve wallmrt aloan - itsa gud stor."

"I've got a bit of an embarrassing confession to make of my own. I can't remember whether it was you I asked to let me know what ROFL stood for? In the reply you/she included LOL. I've always been used to using LOL to mean 'lots of love', and realise I've put it in some really inappropriate places! e.g. 'My heart goes out to you with this tragedy.' LOL"

"N's are stuck on perfection. If your feet aren't perfect they are devalued. You may as well have the feet of an elephant. Ask him why you can smell his ass from across the room. That'll shut him up."

"Try installing a poor-man's security system. Go to a second-hand store, buy a pair of men's used work boots – a really big pair. Put them outside your front door on top of a copy of Guns and Ammunition. Put a dog dish beside it. A really big dog dish. Leave a note on your front door that says something like 'Bubba, big Mike and I have gone to get more ammunition – back in ½ an hour. Don't disturb the Pitbulls, they've just been wormed."

"N said: 'You can't have my mobile phone number because it's private, but I'll need yours so that I can check up where you are at any time.'"

"N said: 'Well, that's enough talk about me. What do you think about me?'"

"N said: 'You'll never find anyone better than me.'"

"N said (to the slow cars in front of him): 'Can't they go any faster, don't they know who I AM!!!'"

"N said: 'A lie is as good as the truth if you can get someone to believe it.'"

"My suggestion, tell him: 'You know, how they say that size doesn't matter? I am sorry to inform you that indeed, it does.'"

"He was the only man I ever knew that could strut while sitting down."

"Every man wants a woman he can look down on."

"There's nothing wrong with narcissists that reasoning with them won't aggravate."

"I'm sorry I didn't get to tell him to screw himself when I had him on the phone. Knowing him, he'd spend hours e-mailing himself trying to seduce himself into getting it done!!!"

"He lied like a dog. Oops, I take that back. That would be insulting to the dog."

"Honey, I just wanted to say you look wonderful while you scream at me that way."

"Does this mean you're about to rage? By the way, would you mind doing something useful while you rage, like getting me a beer and a sandwich?"

"Is this going to be on candid camera? You can't be serious? Where's the hidden camera? (begin looking)"

"I'm thankful for all these little conversations. Without them, I wouldn't know what humility really stands for."

"The new head of the complaint department is Ms. Helen Waite. If you have a complaint, go to Helen Waite."

"I'd love to stay and listen to you talk about yourself, but I gotta run."

"Before you begin, may I adjust your crown?"

"Is there a caboose to your train of thought?"

"They told me you weren't dumb enough to lie all the time. I stuck up for you and said you were."

"I will always cherish the initial misconceptions I had about you."

"I'm really easy to get along with once you people learn to worship me."

"You were sent here as a warning to others, weren't you?"

"Any connection between your reality and mine is purely coincidental."

"100,000 sperm and YOU were the fastest?"

"A narcissist is someone who after taking the trash out, gives the impression he just cleaned the whole house."

"How does a narcissist sleep?
    First he lies on one side, then he lies on the other."

"How can you tell when a narcissist is lying?
    His lips are moving."

"What do you get when you cross the Godfather with a narcissist?
    An offer you can't understand."

"What is the difference between a catfish and a narcissist?
    One's a bottom-crawling scum sucker, and the other's just a fish."

"What do you call an honest narcissist?
   An impossibility."

"Hear about the terrorist that hijacked a 747 full of narcissists?
   He threatened to release one every hour if his demands weren't met."

"What do a narcissist and a sperm have in common?
   Both have about a one in 3 million chance of becoming a human being."

Return

Random Quotes

Search Sam's Web site:

http://samvak.tripod.master.com/texis/master/search/mysite.html

Topical Site Index:

http://www.narcissistic-abuse.com/siteindex.html

"I am very much attracted to vulnerability, to unstable or disordered personalities or to the inferior. Such people constitute more secure sources of better quality Narcissistic Supply. The inferior offer adulation. The mentally disturbed, the traumatised, the abused become dependent and addicted to me. The vulnerable can be easily and economically manipulated without fear of repercussions."

Excerpts from the Archives of the Narcissism List - Part 25 - Sam Vaknin
http://www.geocities.com/vaksam/archive25.html

"If he has a rage attack – rage back. Mirror the narcissist's actions and repeat his words. If he threatens – threaten back and credibly try to use the same language and content. If he leaves the house – leave it as well, disappear on him. If he is suspicious – act suspicious. Be critical, denigrating, humiliating, go down to his level – because that is where he permanently is. Faced with his mirror image – the narcissist always recoils."

How to Cope with a Narcissist? - Sam Vaknin
http://samvak.tripod.com/faq4.html

"The other coping strategy is to give up on him. Abandon him and go about reconstructing your own life. Very few people deserve the kind of investment that is an absolute prerequisite to living with a narcissist. To cope with a narcissist is a full time, energy and emotion-draining job, which reduces the persons around the narcissist to insecure nervous wrecks. Who deserves such a sacrifice? No one, to my mind, not even the most brilliant, charming, breathtaking, suave narcissist. The glamour and trickery wear thin and underneath them a monster lurks which sucks the affect, distorts the cognition and irreversibly influences the lives of those around it for the worse."

How to Cope With a Narcissist? - Sam Vaknin
http://samvak.tripod.com/faq4.html

"Narcissists are incorrigibly and notoriously difficult to change. Thus, trying to change them is doomed to failure. You should either accept them as they are or avoid them altogether. If one accepts the narcissist as he is - one should cater to his needs. His needs are part of what he is. Would you have ignored a physical handicap? Would you not have assisted a quadriplegic? The narcissist is an emotional invalid. He needs constant adulation. He cannot help it. So, if one chooses to accept him - it is a package deal, all his needs included."

How to Cope With a Narcissist? - Sam Vaknin
http://samvak.tripod.com/faq4.html

"The two collaborate in this macabre dance. The narcissist is formed by his partner inasmuch as he forms her. Submission breeds superiority and masochism breeds sadism. The relationships are characterised by rampant emergentism: roles are allocated almost from the start and any deviation meets with an aggressive, even violent reaction."

The Spouse / Mate / Partner of the Narcissist - Sam Vaknin
http://samvak.tripod.com/faq6.html

"The narcissist is never whole without an adoring, submissive, available, self-denigrating partner. His very sense of superiority, indeed his False Self, depends on it."

The Spouse / Mate / Partner of the Narcissist - Sam Vaknin
http://samvak.tripod.com/faq6.html

"If there is anything which can safely be said about those who emotionally team up with narcissists, it is that they are overtly and overly dependent. The partner doesn't know what to do – and this is only too natural in the mayhem that is the relationship with the narcissist. But the typical partner also does not know what she wants and, to a large extent, who she is and what she wants to become."

The Spouse / Mate / Partner of the Narcissist - Sam Vaknin
http://samvak.tripod.com/faq6.html

"The narcissist idealises and then DEVALUES and discards the object of his initial idealisation. This abrupt, heartless devaluation IS abuse. ALL narcissists idealise and then devalue. This is THE core of pathological narcissism. The narcissist exploits, lies, insults, demeans, ignores (the 'silent treatment'), manipulates, controls. All these are forms of abuse."

The Spouse / Mate / Partner of the Narcissist - Sam Vaknin
http://samvak.tripod.com/faq6.html

"If all else fails, the narcissist recruits friends, colleagues, mates, family members, the authorities, institutions, neighbours – in short, third parties – to do his bidding. He uses these them to cajole, coerce, threaten, stalk, offer, retreat, tempt, convince, harass, communicate and otherwise manipulate his target. He controls these unaware instruments exactly as he plans to control his ultimate prey. He employs the same mechanisms and devices. And he dumps his props unceremoniously when the job is done."

The Spouse / Mate / Partner of the Narcissist - Sam Vaknin
http://samvak.tripod.com/faq6.html

"Socially isolating and excluding the victim by discrediting her through a campaign of malicious rumours; harassing the victim by using others to stalk her or by charging her with offences she did not commit; provoking the victim into aggressive or even antisocial conduct by having others threaten her or her loved ones; colluding with others to render the victim dependent on the abuser.
   But, by far, her children are the abuser's greatest source of leverage over his abused spouse or mate."

Abuse by Proxy - Sam Vaknin
http://samvak.tripod.com/abuse11.html

"The abuser perverts the system – therapists, marriage counselours, mediators, court-appointed guardians, police officers, and judges. He uses them to pathologise the victim and to separate her from her sources of emotional sustenance – notably, from her children. The abuser seeks custody to pain his ex and punish her."

Leveraging the Children - Sam Vaknin
http://www.suite101.com/article.cfm/9128/107024

Abuse by Proxy - Sam Vaknin
http://samvak.tripod.com/abuse11.html

"The fostering, propagation and enhancement of an atmosphere of fear, intimidation, instability, unpredictability and irritation. There are no acts of traceable or provable explicit abuse, nor any manipulative settings of control. Yet, the irksome feeling remains, a disagreeable foreboding, a premonition, a bad omen. This is sometimes called "gaslighting". In the long-term, such an environment erodes one's sense of self-worth and self-esteem. Self-confidence is shaken badly. Often, the victims go a paranoid or schizoid and thus are exposed even more to criticism and judgement. The roles are thus reversed: the victim is considered mentally disordered and the narcissist – the suffering soul. What to do? Run! Get away! Ambient abuse often develops to overt and violent abuse. You don't owe anyone an explanation – but you owe yourself a life. Bail out."

The Spouse / Mate / Partner of the Narcissist - Sam Vaknin
http://samvak.tripod.com/faq6.html

"A suspension of judgement is part and parcel of a suspension of individuality, which is both a prerequisite to and the result of living with a narcissist. The partner no longer knows what is true and right, and what is wrong and forbidden. The narcissist recreates for the partner the sort of emotional ambience that led to his formation in the first place: capriciousness, fickleness, arbitrariness, emotional (and physical or sexual) abandonment. The world becomes uncertain and frightening and the partner has only one sure thing to cling to: the narcissist."

The Spouse / Mate / Partner of the Narcissist - Sam Vaknin
http://samvak.tripod.com/faq6.html

"The narcissist rates people around him. First, he conducts a binary test: can this or that person provide him with Narcissistic Supply? As far as the narcissist is concerned, those who fail this simple test do not exist. They are two-dimensional cartoon figures. Their feelings, needs and fears are of no interest or importance."

Exploitation by a Narcissist - Sam Vaknin
http://samvak.tripod.com/faq10.html

"But he has a diminished capacity to empathise, so he rarely feels sorry for what he does. He almost never puts himself in the shoes of his 'victims'."

Is the Narcissist Ever Sorry? - Sam Vaknin
http://samvak.tripod.com/faq14.html

"Question: Many of the symptoms and signs that you describe apply to other personality disorders as well (example: the Histrionic Personality Disorder or the Borderline Personality Disorder). Are we to think that all personality disorders are interrelated?

Answer: Yes, they are interrelated, in my view, at least phenomenologically. We have no Grand Unifying Theory of Psychopathology. We do not know whether there are - and what are - the mechanisms underlying mental disorders. At best, mental health professionals register symptoms (as reported by the patient) and signs (as observed). Then, they group them into syndromes and, more specifically, into disorders. This is descriptive, not explanatory science. Sure, there are a few theories around (psychoanalysis, to mention the most famous) but they all failed miserably at providing a coherent, consistent theoretical framework with predictive powers. Patients suffering from personality disorders have many things in common..."

Other Personality Disorders - Sam Vaknin
http://samvak.tripod.com/faq15.html

"When deprived of Narcissistic Supply - Primary AND Secondary - the narcissist feels annulled. It feels much like being hollowed out, mentally disembowelled or watching oneself die. It is evaporation, disintegration into molecules of terrified anguish, helplessly and inexorably. Without Narcissistic Supply - the narcissist crumbles, like the zombies or the vampires one sees in horror movies. It is terrifying and the narcissist will do anything to avoid it. Think about the narcissist as a drug addict. His withdrawal symptoms are identical: delusions, physiological effects, irritability, emotional lability. Narcissists often experience brief, de-compensatory psychotic episodes when they are disassembled – either in therapy or following a life-crisis accompanied by a major narcissistic injury."

>   The Narcissist's Reaction to Deficient Narcissistic Supply - Sam Vaknin
>   http://samvak.tripod.com/faq28.html

"He mines others for Narcissistic Supply – adulation, attention, reflection, fear."

>   Ideas of Reference - Sam Vaknin
>   http://samvak.tripod.com/journal41.html

"The narcissist looks depressed, his movements slow down, his sleep patterns are disturbed (he either sleeps too much or becomes insomniac), his eating patterns change (he gorges on food or is unable even to look at it). He is be constantly dysphoric (sad), anhedonic (finds no interest in the world, no pleasure in anything or in any of his former pursuits and interests). He is subjected to violent mood swings (mainly rage attacks) and all his (visible and painful) efforts at self-control fail."

>   The Narcissist's Reaction to Deficient Narcissistic Supply - Sam Vaknin
>   http://samvak.tripod.com/faq28.html

"Sex for the narcissist is an instrument designed to increase the number of Sources of Narcissistic Supply. If it happens to be the most efficient weapon in the narcissist's arsenal – he will make profligate use of it. In other words: if the narcissist cannot obtain adoration, admiration, approval, applause, or any other kind of attention by other means (e.g., intellectually) – he resorts to sex. He then become a satyr (or a nymphomaniac): indiscriminately engages in sex with multiple partners. His sex partners are considered by him to be objects not of desire – but of Narcissistic Supply."

>   Narcissists, Sex and Fidelity - Sam Vaknin
>   http://samvak.tripod.com/faq29.html

"His very pursuit of Narcissistic Supply is compulsive. The narcissist seeks to recreate and replay old traumas, ancient, unresolved conflicts with figures of (primary) importance in his life. He feels guilty and that he should be punished. He makes sure that he is. These all possess the tint and hue of compulsion. In many respects, narcissism can be defined as an obsessive-compulsive disorder gone berserk."

The Compulsive Acts of the Narcissist - Sam Vaknin
http://samvak.tripod.com/faq30.html

"Where the regular compulsive patient feels that the compulsive act restores his control over himself and over his life – the narcissist feels that the compulsive act restores his control over his environment and secures his future Narcissistic Supply."

The Compulsive Acts of the Narcissist - Sam Vaknin
http://samvak.tripod.com/faq30.html

"Losing the narcissist is no different to any other major loss in life. It provokes a cycle of bereavement and grief (as well as some kind of mild Post-Traumatic Stress Syndrome in cases of severe abuse). This cycle has four phases: denial, rage, sadness and acceptance. Some people, however, cannot get past the denial, or rage phases. They remain 'stuck', frozen in time, constantly replaying mental tapes of the interactions they had with the narcissists. What they don't realise is that these tapes are 'foreign objects' implanted by the narcissist in their mind. Time bombs waiting to explode. Kind of 'sleeper cells' or post-hypnotic suggestion. If you find yourself in this situation there is little you can do to help yourself. You need professional assistance."

Excerpts from the Archives of the Narcissism List - Part 40 - Sam Vaknin
http://samvak.tripod.com/archive40.html

"They are a loose terror-based coalition between a sadistic, idealised Superego and a grandiose and manipulative False Ego. Their interactions are mechanical. They are Narcissistic Supply seeking robots. No robot is capable of introspection."

Narcissists and Introspection - Sam Vaknin
http://samvak.tripod.com/faq49.html

"Narcissism is contagious. The narcissism creates a 'bubble universe', similar to a cult. In this bubble, special rules apply. These rules do not always correspond to outer reality. Using complex defence mechanisms, such as Projective Identification, the narcissist forces his victims – spouse, mate, friend, colleague – to 'play a role' assigned to him by 'God' – the narcissist. The narcissist rewards compliance with his script and punishes any deviation from it with severe abuse. In other words, the narcissist CONDITIONS people around him using intimidation, positive and negative reinforcements and feedback, ambient abuse ('gaslighting'), covert, or controlling abuse, and overt, classical abuse. Thus conditioned, the narcissist's victims gradually come to assimilate the narcissist's way of thinking (follies a-deux) and his modus operandi – his methods. You can abandon the narcissist – but the narcissist never abandons you. He is there, deep inside your traumatic memories, lurking, waiting to act out. You have been modified, very much like an alien snatching bodies."

Excerpts from the Archives of the Narcissism List – Part 40 – Sam Vaknin
http://samvak.tripod.com/archive40.html

"The narcissist needs his parents alive mostly in order to get back at them, to accuse and punish them for what they have done to him. This attempt at reciprocity ('settling the scores') represents to him justice and order, it introduces sense and logic into an otherwise totally confused landscape. It is a triumph of right over wrong, weak over strong, law and order over chaos and capriciousness. The demise of his parents is perceived by him to be a cosmic joke at his expense. He feels 'stuck' for the rest of his life with the consequences of events and behaviour not of his own doing or fault. The villains evade responsibility by leaving the stage, ignoring the script and the director's (the narcissist's) orders. The narcissist goes through a final big cycle of helpless rage when his parents die."

The Dead Parents – Sam Vaknin
http://samvak.tripod.com/faq54.html

"The narcissist should take responsibility for his life and not relegate it to some hitherto rather obscure psychodynamic concept. This is the first and most important step to healing."

Reconditioning the Narcissist – Sam Vaknin
http://samvak.tripod.com/faq63.html

"Question: I write to you because in your writing, you seem to be very sceptical that the individual with a Narcissistic Personality Disorder can be treated successfully. Is that your position?

Answer: No, it is the position of clinical psychologists (which I am NOT) who bothered to write about the subject."

Reconditioning the Narcissist - Sam Vaknin
http://samvak.tripod.com/faq63.html

"To 'qualify' as an inverted narcissist - you must CRAVE to be in a relationship with a narcissist, regardless of any abuse inflicted on you by him/her. You must ACTIVELY seek relationships with narcissists - and ONLY with narcissists - no matter what your (bitter and traumatic) past experience has been. You must feel EMPTY and UNHAPPY in relationships with ANY OTHER kind of person. Only THEN - AND if you satisfy the other diagnostic criteria of a Dependent Personality Disorder - can you be safely labelled an 'inverted narcissist'."

The Inverted Narcissist - Sam Vaknin
http://samvak.tripod.com/faq66.html

"If your narcissist is cerebral and NOT interested in having much sex - then give yourself ample permission to have sex with other people. Your cerebral narcissist will not be indifferent to infidelity so discretion and secrecy is of paramount importance."

The Inverted Narcissist - Sam Vaknin
http://samvak.tripod.com/faq66.html

"FINALLY, and most important of all for the inverted narcissist: KNOW YOURSELF. What are you getting from the relationship? Are you actually a masochist?"

The Inverted Narcissist - Sam Vaknin
http://samvak.tripod.com/faq66.html

"One can easily manipulate the moods of a narcissist by making a disparaging remark, by disagreeing with him, by criticising him, by doubting his grandiosity or fantastic claims, etc. Such REACTIVE mood shifts have nothing to do with blood sugar levels, which are cyclical. It is possible to reduce the narcissist to a state of rage and depression AT ANY MOMENT, simply by employing the above 'technique'. He can be elated, even manic – and in a split second, following a narcissistic injury, depressed, sulking or raging."

> Narcissists and Chemical Imbalances - Sam Vaknin
> http://samvak.tripod.com/faq70.html

"Additionally, the narcissist goes through mega-cycles which last months or even years."

> Narcissists and Chemical Imbalances - Sam Vaknin
> http://samvak.tripod.com/faq70.html

"Narcissists VERY rarely commit suicide. It runs against the grain. They have suicidal ideation and reactive psychoses under severe stress – but to commit suicide runs against the grain of narcissism. This is more of a Borderline Personality Disorder trait."

> Myths about Narcissism - Sam Vaknin
> http://samvak.tripod.com/faq72.html

"Of course narcissists love to have an audience. But they love an audience only because and as long as it provides them with Narcissistic Supply. Otherwise, they are not interested in human beings (they lack empathy which makes other humans much less fascinating than they are to empathic people).

Narcissists are terrified of introspection. I am not referring to intellectualisation or rationalisation or simple application of their intelligence – this would not constitute introspection. Proper introspection must include an emotional element, an insight and the ability to emotionally integrate the insight so that it affects behaviour. Some people are narcissists and they KNOW it (cognitively). They even think about it from time to time – is this introspection? Not really. Narcissists do engage in real introspection following a life crisis, though. They attend therapy at such time."

> Myths about Narcissism - Sam Vaknin
> http://samvak.tripod.com/faq72.html

"In response to a life crisis (divorce, disgrace, imprisonment, accident and severe narcissistic injuries) the narcissist is likely to adopt either of two reactions:

1. He finally refers himself to therapy, realising that something is dangerously wrong with him. Statistics show that talk therapies are rather ineffective when it comes to narcissists. Soon enough, the therapist is bored, fed up or actively repelled by the grandiose fantasies and open contempt of the narcissist. The therapeutic alliance crumbles and the narcissist emerges 'triumphant' having sucked the therapist's energy dry.
2. He frantically gropes for alternative Sources of Narcissistic Supply. Narcissists are very creative. If all fails, they exhibitionistically make use of their own misery. Or they lie, create a fantasy, invent stories, harp on other people's emotions, forge a medical condition, pull a stunt, fall in ideal love with the chief nurse, make a provocative move or a crime. The narcissist is bound to come up with a surprising angle.

Experience shows that most narcissists go through (1) and then through (2)."

Myths about Narcissism - Sam Vaknin
http://samvak.tripod.com/faq72.html

"Where is love in all this? Where is the commitment to the loved one's welfare, the discipline, the extension of oneself to incorporate the beloved, the mutual growth? Nowhere to be seen."

The Two Loves of the Narcissist - Sam Vaknin
http://samvak.tripod.com/journal69.html

"The second 'myth' is that narcissism is a pure phenomenon that can be dealt with experimentally. This is not the case. Actually, due to the fuzziness of the whole field, diagnosticians are both forced AND encouraged to render multiple diagnoses ('co-morbidity'). NPD usually appears in tandem with some other Cluster B disorder (such as Antisocial Personality Disorder, Histrionic Personality Disorder or, most often, Borderline Personality Disorder)."

Myths about Narcissism - Sam Vaknin
http://samvak.tripod.com/faq72.html

"I believe that there is a continuum between families of mental health disorders. I believe that HPD (the Histrionic Personality

Disorder) is actually NPD where the Narcissistic Supply is sex or physique. I think that BPD (Borderline Personality Disorder) is a form of NPD with emphasis on abandonment issues. I think that AsPD (Antisocial Personality Disorder) is NPD with deficient impulse control. I think that pathological narcissism underlies all these – wrongly distinguished – disorders. This is why my book is entitled NARCISSISM Revisited and not NPD."

Myths about Narcissism - Sam Vaknin
http://samvak.tripod.com/faq72.html

"The exposure of the False Self for what it is – False – is a major narcissistic injury. The narcissist is likely to react with severe self-deprecation and self-flagellation even to the point of suicidal ideation. This – on the inside. On the outside, he is likely to react aggressively. This is his way of channelling his life-threatening aggression. Rather than endure its assault and its frightening outcomes – he redirects the aggression, transforms it and hurls it at others. What form his aggression might assume is nigh impossible to predict without knowing the narcissist in question intimately. It could be anything from cynical humour, through brutal honesty, verbal abuse, passive aggressive behaviours (frustrating others) and down to actual physical violence."

Myths about Narcissism - Sam Vaknin
http://samvak.tripod.com/faq72.html

Excerpts from the Archives of the Narcissism List - Part 10 - Sam Vaknin
http://samvak.tripod.com/archive10.html

"Narcissists live in a state of constant rage, repressed aggression, envy and hatred. They firmly believe that everyone is like them. As a result, they are paranoid, suspicious, scared and erratic. Frightening the narcissist is a powerful behaviour modification tool. If sufficiently deterred – the narcissist promptly disengages, gives up everything he was fighting for and sometimes make amends. To act effectively, one has to identify the vulnerabilities and susceptibilities of the narcissist and strike repeated, escalating blows at them – until the narcissist lets go and vanishes.

You don't have to do much except utter a vague reference, make an ominous allusion, delineate a possible turn of events. The narcissist will do the rest for you. He is like a little child in the dark, generating the very monsters that paralyse him with fear. Needless to add that all these activities have to be pursued legally, preferably through the good services of law offices and in broad daylight. If done in the wrong way – they might constitute extortion or blackmail, harassment and a host of other criminal offences."

Vindictive Narcissists - Sam Vaknin
http://samvak.tripod.com/faq75.html

"The other way to neutralise a vindictive narcissist is to offer him continued Narcissistic Supply until the war is over and won by you. Dazzled by the drug of Narcissistic Supply, the narcissist immediately becomes tamed, forgets his vindictiveness and triumphantly takes over his 'property' and 'territory'.

Under the influence of Narcissistic Supply, the narcissist is unable to tell when he is being manipulated. He is blind, dumb and deaf. You can make a narcissist do anything by offering, withholding, or threatening to withhold Narcissistic Supply (adulation, admiration, attention, sex, awe, subservience, etc.)"

Vindictive Narcissists - Sam Vaknin
http://samvak.tripod.com/faq75.html

"I agree that the best way to treat a narcissist is to out-narcissise him/her. Treat it like it treats you and it will vanish in a puff of smoke quicker than a witch. Narcissists are not interested – nor are they sufficiently resilient – to face opposition, disagreement, friction, conflict, in short: negative narcissistic supplies."

Excerpts from the Archives of the Narcissism List - Part 1 - Sam Vaknin
http://samvak.tripod.com/archive1.html

"Even quarrelling with people constitutes NS. Perhaps not the fighting itself – but the ability to influence other people, to induce feelings in them, to manipulate them emotionally, to make them do something or refrain from doing it."

Narcissists, Narcissistic Supply and Sources of Supply - Sam Vaknin
http://samvak.tripod.com/faq76.html

"Narcissists invariably react with narcissistic rage to narcissistic injury.
These two terms bear clarification:
Narcissistic injury

1. Any threat (real or imagined) to the narcissist's grandiose and fantastic self-perception (False Self) as perfect, omnipotent, omniscient, and entitled to special treatment and recognition, regardless of his actual accomplishments (or lack thereof).
2. The narcissist actively solicits Narcissistic Supply - adulation, compliments, admiration, subservience, attention, being feared - from others in order to sustain his fragile and dysfunctional Ego. Thus, he constantly courts possible rejection, criticism, disagreement, and even mockery.

The narcissist is, therefore, dependent on other people. He is aware of the risks associated with such all-pervasive and essential dependence. He resents his weakness and dreads possible disruptions in the flow of his drug - Narcissistic Supply. He is caught between the rock of his habit and the hard place of his frustration. No wonder he is prone to raging, lashing and acting out, and to pathological, all-consuming envy (all expressions of pent-up aggression).

The narcissist is constantly on the lookout for slights. He is hypervigilant. He perceives every disagreement as criticism and every critical remark as complete and humiliating rejection - nothing short of a threat. Gradually, his mind turns into a chaotic battlefield of paranoia and ideas of reference.

Most narcissists react defensively. They become conspicuously indignant, aggressive, and cold. They detach emotionally for fear of yet another (narcissistic) injury. They devalue the person who made the disparaging remark, the critical comment, the unflattering observation, the innocuous joke at the narcissist's expense.

By holding the critic in contempt, by diminishing the stature of the discordant conversant - the narcissist minimises the impact of the disagreement or criticism on himself. This is a defence mechanism known as cognitive dissonance."

The Intermittent Explosive Narcissist - Sam Vaknin
http://samvak.tripod.com/journal86.html

"He seeks out his old Sources of Narcissistic Supply when he has absolutely no other NS Sources at his disposal. Narcissists frantically try to recycle their old and wasted sources in such a situation. But the narcissist would NOT do even this had he not felt that he could still successfully extract a modicum of NS from the old source (even to attack the narcissist is to recognise his existence and to attend to him!!!). If you are an old Source of Narcissistic Supply, first, get over the excitement of seeing him again. It may be flattering, perhaps sexually arousing. Try to overcome these feelings. Then, simply ignore him. Don't bother to respond in any way to his offer to get together. If he talks to you - keep quiet, don't answer. If he calls you - listen politely and then say goodbye and hang up. Indifference is what the narcissist cannot stand. It indicates a lack of attention and interest that constitutes the kernel of negative NS."

Narcissists, Narcissistic Supply and Sources of Supply - Sam Vaknin
http://samvak.tripod.com/faq76.html

"Any statement or fact, which seems to contradict his inflated perception of his grandiose self. Any criticism, disagreement, exposure of fake achievements, belittling of 'talents and skills' which the narcissist fantasises that he possesses, any hint that he is subordinated, subjugated, controlled, owned or dependent upon a third party. Any description of the narcissist as average and common, indistinguishable from many others. Any hint that the narcissist is weak, needy, dependent, deficient, slow, not intelligent, naive, gullible, susceptible, not in the know, manipulated, a victim. The narcissist is likely to react with rage to all these and, in an effort to re-establish his fantastic grandiosity, he is likely to expose facts and stratagems he had no conscious intention of exposing."

The Narcissist in Court - Sam Vaknin
http://samvak.tripod.com/faq78.html

"Narcissists are misogynists. They team up with women as mere Sources of SNS (Secondary Narcissistic Supply). The woman's chores are to accumulate past NS and release it in an orderly manner, so as to regulate the fluctuating flow of Primary Supply."

Narcissists and Women - Sam Vaknin
http://samvak.tripod.com/faq79.html

"To live with a narcissist is an arduous and eroding task. Narcissists are atrabilious, infinitely pessimistic, bad-tempered, paranoid and sadistic in an absent-minded and indifferent manner. Their daily routine is a rigmarole of threats, complaints, hurts, eruptions, moodiness and rage. The N rails against slights true and imagined.

He alienates people. He humiliates them because this is his only weapon against the humiliation of their indifference."

           Narcissists and Women - Sam Vaknin
             http://samvak.tripod.com/faq79.html

"Narcissists are angry men – but not because they never experienced love and probably never will. They are angry because they are not as powerful, awe inspiring and successful as they wish they were and, to their mind, deserve to be."

           Narcissists and Women - Sam Vaknin
             http://samvak.tripod.com/faq79.html

"PDs have so MANY things in common that serious authorities have been questioning the individual existence of this or that PD (including BPD) ever since the 1980s."

  Excerpts from the Archives of the Narcissism List - Part 4 - Sam Vaknin
             http://samvak.tripod.com/archive04.html

"Thus, to invest in a narcissist is a purposeless, futile and meaningless activity. To the narcissist, every day is a new beginning, a hunt, a new cycle of idealisation or devaluation, a newly invented self. There is no accumulation of credits or goodwill because the narcissist has no past and no future. He occupies an eternal and timeless present. He is a fossil caught in the frozen lava of a volcanic childhood. The narcissist does not keep agreements, does not adhere to laws, regards consistency and predictability as demeaning traits."

          The Discontinuous Narcissist - Sam Vaknin
            http://samvak.tripod.com/journal20.html

"This false information and the informative asymmetry in the relationship guarantee his informative lead, or 'advantage'. This is an active state of dis-intimisation and dis-information, which casts a pall of cover up, separateness, asymmetry and mystery over the narcissist's relationships. The narcissist lies even in therapy. In encounters with professionals of all kinds, he uses professional lingo to "belong" to this unique class of people and to the most unique group of all: the Renaissance Men. By demonstrating his control of several professional jargons he almost proves (to himself) that he is superhuman."

Uniqueness and Intimacy - Sam Vaknin
http://samvak.tripod.com/msla2.html

"There is no way out of the narcissistic catch: the narcissist despises, in equal measures, both the submissive and the independent, the strong (who constitute a threat) and the weak (who are, by definition, despicable)."

Uniqueness and Intimacy - Sam Vaknin
http://samvak.tripod.com/msla2.html

"The narcissist anticipates his abandonment and, paradoxically, by trying to avoid it, he precipitates it. Maybe he does that on purpose: after all, if he is the cause of his own abandonment - surely he is in control of his own relationships. To be in control - this unconquerable drive - is the direct result of being deserted, neglected, avoided, or abused at an early stage in life. 'Never again' - vows the narcissist - 'If anyone will do the leaving, it will be me.'"

Uniqueness and Intimacy - Sam Vaknin
http://samvak.tripod.com/msla2.html

"The shift from benevolent lover-partner to a raging maniac with a total lack of empathy - is terrifying. The transformation is so complete that a 'Dr. Jekyll and Mr. Hyde' effect is created."

Uniqueness and Intimacy - Sam Vaknin
http://samvak.tripod.com/msla2.html

"But he does not need companionship, emotional support, let alone true partnership. There is no beast on earth more self-sufficient than a narcissist. Years of unpredictability in his relationships with meaningful others, early on abuse, sometimes decades of violence, aggression, instability and humiliation - have eroded the narcissist's trust in others to the point of disappearance. The narcissist knows that he can rely only on one stable, unconditional source of love: himself."

Uniqueness and Intimacy - Sam Vaknin
http://samvak.tripod.com/msla2.html

"I am often shocked when presented with incontrovertible evidence to an event in my past, something I said, or did, a person I knew, a sentence I have written. I do not remember having done, said, or written what is attributed to me. I do not recall having met the person, having felt anything, having been there. It is not that it looks alien to me, as though it happened to someone else. I simply have no recollection whatsoever, I draw a blank. Hence my enormous and recurrent and terrifyingly helpless state of surprise. These cognitive distortions, these lapses of memory are as close as I ever get to losing control."

Being There - Sam Vaknin
http://samvak.tripod.com/journal32.html

"Before I meet someone, I learn everything I can about him. I then proceed to acquire superficial knowledge that is certain to create the impression of genius bordering on omniscience. If I am to meet a politician from Turkey, whose hobby is farming, and is the author of books about ancient pottery - I will while away days and nights studying Turkish history, ancient pottery, and farming. Not an hour after the meeting - having inspired awesome admiration in my new acquaintance - all the facts I so meticulously memorised evaporate, never to return. The original views I expressed so confidently vanish from my mind. I am preoccupied with my next prey and with his predilections and interests."

Being There - Sam Vaknin
http://samvak.tripod.com/journal32.html

"It is the fact that language is put by narcissists to a different use - not to communicate but to obscure, not to share but to abstain, not to learn but to defend and resist, not to teach but to preserve ever less tenable monopolies, to disagree without incurring wrath, to criticise without commitment, to agree without appearing to do so. Thus, an 'agreement' with a narcissist is a vague expression of intent at a given moment - rather than the clear listing of long-term, iron-cast and mutual commitments."

The Weapon of Language - Sam Vaknin
http://samvak.tripod.com/journal34.html

"With the classic narcissist, language is used cruelly and ruthlessly to ensnare one's enemies, to saw confusion and panic, to move others to emulate the narcissist (Projective Identification), to leave the listeners in doubt, in hesitation, in paralysis, to gain control, or to punish."

The Weapon of Language - Sam Vaknin
http://samvak.tripod.com/journal34.html

"The narcissist prefers to wait and see and see what waiting brings. It is the postponement of the inevitable that leads to the inevitability of postponement as a strategy of survival."

The Weapon of Language - Sam Vaknin
http://samvak.tripod.com/journal34.html

"They are avoided and ignored, rendered transparent by their checkered past. They are passed over for promotion, never invited to professional or social gatherings, cold-shouldered by the media. They are snubbed and disregarded. They are never the recipients of perks, benefits, or awards. They are blamed when not blameworthy and rarely praised when deserving. They are being constantly and consistently punished for who they were. It is poetic justice in more than one way. They are being treated narcissistically by their erstwhile victims. They finally are tasting their own medicine, the bitter harvest of their wrath and arrogance."

To Age with Grace - Sam Vaknin
http://samvak.tripod.com/journal54.html

"Narcissists are aided, abetted and facilitated by four types of people and institutions: the adulators, the blissfully ignorant, the self-deceiving and those deceived by the narcissist."

Facilitating Narcissism - Sam Vaknin
http://samvak.tripod.com/journal62.html

"'If only he tried hard enough', 'If he only really wanted to heal', 'If only we found the right therapy', 'If only his defences were down', 'There MUST be something good and worthy under the hideous façade', 'NO ONE can be that evil and destructive', 'He must have meant it differently', 'God, or a higher being, or the spirit, or the soul is the solution and the answer to our prayers'. The narcissist holds such thinking in barely undisguised contempt. To him, it is a sign of weakness, the scent of prey, a gaping vulnerability. He uses and abuses this human need for order, good, and meaning – as he uses and abuses all other human needs. Gullibility, selective blindness, malignant optimism – these are the weapons of the beast. And the abused are hard at work to provide it with its arsenal."

The Malignant Optimism of the Abused – Sam Vaknin
http://samvak.tripod.com/journal27.html

"The Pollyanna defences of the abused are aimed against the emerging and horrible understanding that humans are specks of dust in a totally indifferent Universe, the playthings of evil and sadistic forces, of which the narcissist is one – as well as against the unbearable realisation that their pain means nothing to anyone but themselves. Nothing whatsoever. It has all been in vain."

The Malignant Optimism of the Abused – Sam Vaknin
http://samvak.tripod.com/journal27.html

"But the narcissist is rarely there to watch his invaded victims writhe and suffer. At the first sign of trouble, he flees and disappears. This act of vanishing need not be physical or geographical. The narcissist is better at disappearing emotionally and at evading his legal obligations (despite constant righteous moralising). It is then and there that the people who surround the narcissist discover his true colours: he uses and discards people in an absentminded manner. To him, people are either 'functional' and 'useful' in his pursuit of Narcissistic Supply – or not human at all, dimensionless cartoons. Of all the hurts that the narcissist can inflict – this, probably, is the strongest and most enduring one."

Narcissism by Proxy – Sam Vaknin
http://samvak.tripod.com/faq42.html

"Even the victim's relatives, friends, and colleagues are amenable to the considerable charm, persuasiveness, and manipulativeness of the abuser and to his impressive thespian skills. The abuser offers a plausible rendition of the events and interprets them to his favour. Others rarely have a chance to witness an abusive exchange first hand and at close quarters. In contrast, the victims are often on the verge of a nervous breakdown: harassed, unkempt, irritable, impatient, abrasive, and hysterical."

Narcissism by Proxy - Sam Vaknin
http://samvak.tripod.com/faq42.html

"The narcissist's inadequacies are so glaring and his denial and other defence mechanisms so primitive – that we feel like constantly screaming at him, berating, debasing and reproaching him, even to the point of striking at him literally as well as figuratively. Ashamed at these reactions, we begin to also feel guilty. We find ourselves attached to a mental pendulum, swinging between repulsion and guilt, rage and pity, lack of empathy and remorse. Slowly we acquire the very characteristics of the narcissist that we so deplore."

Narcissism by Proxy - Sam Vaknin
http://samvak.tripod.com/faq42.html

"Having made them compatible with his own disorder, having secured the submission of his victims – he moves on to occupy their shells. Then he makes them do what he always dreamt of doing, what he often desired, what he constantly feared of. Using the same compelling methods, he drives his mates, spouse, partners, colleagues, children, or co-workers – into collaborating in the expression of the repressed side of his personality. At the same time, he negates the vague sensation that their personality has been substituted by his when committing these acts.

The narcissist can, thus, derive, vicariously, through the lives of others, the Narcissistic Supply that he so needs. He induces in them criminal, romantic, heroic impulses. He navigates them to forbidden realms of the intellect. He makes them travel far, travel fast, travel light, behave against all norms, gamble against all odds, fear not – in short: be what he could never be. The narcissist thrives on the attention, admiration, fascination, or horrified reactions lavished upon his proxies. He consumes the Narcissistic Supply flowing through these human conduits of his own making."

Narcissism by Proxy - Sam Vaknin
http://samvak.tripod.com/faq42.html

"The narcissist devours people, consumes their output, and casts the empty, writhing shells aside."

>That Thing Between a Man and a Woman - Sam Vaknin
>http://samvak.tripod.com/journal26.html

"Most narcissists reject the notion or diagnosis that they are mentally disturbed."

>The Narcissist in Love - Sam Vaknin
>http://samvak.tripod.com/journal15.html

"Where normal people love others and empathise with them, the narcissist loves his False Self and identifies with it to the exclusion of all else – his True Self included."

>The Narcissist in Love - Sam Vaknin
>http://samvak.tripod.com/journal15.html

"Money and possessions represent power, they are love substitutes, they are movable or disposable on short notice. They constitute an inseparable part of a PNS and form a determinant of FEGO. The narcissist assimilates them and identifies with them. This is why he is so traumatised by their loss or depreciation. They provide him with the certainty and security that he feels nowhere else. They are familiar, predictable, and controllable. There is no danger involved in emotionally investing in them."

>Malignant Self Love Narcissism Revisited - Sam Vaknin
>http://samvak.tripod.com/msla8.html

"In my view, the function of Narcissistic Accumulation is equivalent to the replacement of objects. This means that narcissists live with their spouse only as long as she fully caters to their narcissistic needs through accumulation and adoration. His misogyny and his sadism are a result of his fear of being abandoned (the recreation of earlier traumas) and not a result of narcissism. A narcissist with an ideal, sadistic, rigid, primitive, and punishing Superego inevitably becomes antisocial and lacking in morals and in conscience."

>Malignant Self Love Narcissism Revisited - Sam Vaknin
>http://samvak.tripod.com/msla8.html

"The narcissist treats women the way he does in order to weaken them and to make them dependent on him so as to prevent them from abandoning him. He uses a variety of techniques to pulverise all their foci of strength: a healthy sexuality, family, career, self-esteem and self-image, mental health, reality test, and social circles. Once devoid of all these, he remains their only available source of authority, interest, meaning, feeling and hope. A woman thus deprived will be highly unlikely to leave him. This state of emotional addiction is created by unpredictable behaviours, which cause reactions of fear and phobic hesitation. The Misogynist, on the other hand, hates women, humiliates them, scorns them and despises them.

They must not be garrulous, they must be slow, inferior in some important respect, submissive, with an aesthetic appearance, intelligent but passive, admiring (accumulator), emotionally available, dependent and either simple or femme fatale. They are not his type if they are critical, express disagreement, demonstrate superiority, sophistication, independent, or provide unsolicited advice or opinions. The narcissist forms no relationships with such women."

Malignant Self Love Narcissism Revisited - Sam Vaknin
http://samvak.tripod.com/msla8.html

"Having spotted the 'right profile' the narcissist proceeds to see if he is sexually attracted to the woman. If he is, he proceeds to condition her using a variety of measures: sex, money, assumption of responsibilities, fostering sexual, emotional, existential and operational uncertainties (followed by bouts of relief on her part as conflicts are resolved), grandiose gestures, expressions of interest, of need and of dependence (mistakenly interpreted by the woman to mean deep emotions), grandiose plans, idealisation, demonstrations of unlimited trust (but no sharing of decision making powers), encouraging feelings of uniqueness and of pseudo-intimacy, and childlike behaviour. Dependence is formed and a new SNSS is born."

Malignant Self Love Narcissism Revisited - Sam Vaknin
http://samvak.tripod.com/msla8.html

"If she is interested only in sex, it means that she perceives the narcissist merely as a sex object and thus she totally negates his uniqueness. He is likely to panic and keep his distance from this expressly anti-narcissistic agent."

       Malignant Self Love Narcissism Revisited - Sam Vaknin
       http://samvak.tripod.com/msla8.html

"The narcissist constantly clashed with figures of authority because he feels entitled to special treatment, immune to prosecution and superior."

       The Workings of the Narcissist - Sam Vaknin
       http://samvak.tripod.com/msla3to4.html

"Mostly, the narcissist prefers to be feared or admired – rather than loved."

       The Workings of the Narcissist - Sam Vaknin
       http://samvak.tripod.com/msla3to4.html

"The narcissist is, thus, often described by others as 'robotic', 'machine', 'inhuman', 'emotionless' and so on. People are deterred by his emotional absence. They are wary of him and keep their guard up at all times."

     The Tortured Self - The Inner World of the Narcissist - Sam Vaknin
       http://samvak.tripod.com/msla3to4.html

"But, the narcissist abuses people. He misleads them into believing that they mean something to him, that they are special and dear to him, and that he cares about them. When they discover that it was all a charade, they are likely to respond much more forcefully than is usual."

     The Tortured Self - The Inner World of the Narcissist - Sam Vaknin
       http://samvak.tripod.com/msla3to4.html

"Narcissists cannot delay gratification. They are creatures of the here and now, because they judge themselves to be all deserving. When forced to specialise or persist – they develop a feeling of stagnation and death. It is not the result of a choice – rather, it is a structural constraint. This is the way a narcissist is built, this is his modus operandi, and his vacillating style of life and array of activities, are written into his operations manual. A direct result of this is that a narcissist cannot form a stable marital relationship, reasonably devote himself to his family, maintain an on going business, reside in one place for long, dedicate himself to a profession or to a career, complete academic studies, or accumulate material wealth. Narcissists are often described as unstable, unreliable, unable to undertake long-term commitments and obligations, or to maintain a job, or a career path. The narcissist's life is characterised by jerky, episodic careers, relationships, marriages, and domiciles."

The Tortured Self - The Inner World of the Narcissist - Sam Vaknin
http://samvak.tripod.com/msla3to4.html

"The narcissist's behaviour is experienced by his mate as frustrating and growth-cramping. To live with him is akin to living with a non-entity, with dead or dormant qualities. The partners of the narcissist often describe a feeling of imprisonment and punishment."

Uniqueness and Intimacy - Sam Vaknin
http://samvak.tripod.com/msla2.html

"The narcissist is devoid of empathy and incapable of intimacy with others as well as with himself. To him, lying has become a second nature. An alter (False) Ego soon takes over. He begins to believe his own lies. He makes himself out to be what he wants to be and not what he is."

Uniqueness and Intimacy - Sam Vaknin
http://samvak.tripod.com/msla2.html

"He ultimately abhors his children and tries to limit and confine them to the role of Narcissistic Supply Sources."

Uniqueness and Intimacy - Sam Vaknin
http://samvak.tripod.com/msla2.html

"The more severe cases of Narcissistic Personality Disorders (NPD) display partial control of their drives, anxiety intolerance and rigid sublimatory channels. With these individuals, the magnitude of the hatred is so great, that they deny both the emotion and any awareness of it. Alternatively, aggression is converted to action or to acting out. This denial affects normal cognitive functioning as well. Such an individual would, intermittently, have bouts of arrogance, curiosity and pseudo-stupidity, all transformations of aggression taken to the extreme. It is difficult to tell envy from hatred in these cases."

Uniqueness and Intimacy - Sam Vaknin
http://samvak.tripod.com/msla2.html

"The more intimate the relationship, the more the other party has to lose by severing it, the more dependent the narcissist's partner is on the relationship and on the narcissist - the more likely is the narcissist to be aggressive, hostile, envious, and hating. This serves a dual function: as an outlet for pent up aggression - and as a kind of test."

Uniqueness and Intimacy - Sam Vaknin
http://samvak.tripod.com/msla2.html

"The narcissist concludes that if people choose to hang on to their relationships with him despite his despicable, intolerable behaviour - than he must be as unique and precious as he feels himself to be."

Uniqueness and Intimacy - Sam Vaknin
http://samvak.tripod.com/msla2.html

"The narcissist dedicates a lot of his time and energy to a debate, which rages inside him and which revolves around two axes: (a) is he unique and (b) if so, to what extent and how can this be substantiated, communicated and documented?"

Being Special - Sam Vaknin
http://samvak.tripod.com/msla1.html

"The narcissist creates two masks, which serve to hide him from the world - and to extract from the world his needs and desires."

The Emotional Involvement Preventive Measures - Sam Vaknin
http://samvak.tripod.com/msla8.html

"In the narcissist's surrealistic world, even language is pathologised. It mutates into a weapon of self-defence, a verbal fortification, a medium without a message, replacing words with duplicitous and ambiguous vocables. Narcissists (and, often, by contagion, their unfortunate victims) don't talk, or communicate. They fend off. They hide and evade and avoid and disguise."

The Weapon of Language - Sam Vaknin
http://samvak.tripod.com/journal34.html

"Narcissists, therefore, never talk to others – rather, they talk at others, or lecture them. They exchange subtexts, camouflage-wrapped by elaborate, florid, texts. They read between the lines, spawning a multitude of private languages, prejudices, superstitions, conspiracy theories, rumours, phobias and hysterias. Theirs is a solipsistic world – where communication is permitted only with oneself and the aim of language is to throw others off the scent or to obtain Narcissistic Supply."

The Weapon of Language - Sam Vaknin
http://samvak.tripod.com/journal34.html

"The narcissist is too important to pay attention to day to day chores. He is also infallible. Any time he commits an error, has bad luck, exerts the wrong judgment, or, simply, has to face a task – the narcissist 'passes the buck'. People close to him are to blame. They did not pay attention, they did not alert him on time, they did not prevent what happened, or did not notice the importance of what he was doing, did not make his life easier (after all, this is their raison d'etre)."

Loss of Control of Grandiosity - Sam Vaknin
http://samvak.tripod.com/msla9.html

"Pathological narcissism is founded on alloplastic defences – the firm conviction that the world or others are to blame for one's behaviour. The narcissist firmly believes that people around him should be held responsible for his reactions or have triggered them. With such a state of mind so firmly entrenched, the narcissist is incapable of admitting that something is wrong with HIM."

The Narcissist in Love - Sam Vaknin
http://samvak.tripod.com/journal15.html

"But that is not to say that the narcissist does not experience his disorder. He does. But he re-interprets this experience. He regards his dysfunctional behaviours – social, sexual, emotional, mental – as conclusive and irrefutable proof of his superiority, brilliance, distinction, prowess, might, or success. Rudeness to others is reinterpreted as efficiency. Abusive behaviours are cast as educational. Sexual absence as proof of preoccupation with higher functions. His rage is always just and a reaction to injustice or being misunderstood by intellectual dwarves."

The Narcissist in Love - Sam Vaknin
http://samvak.tripod.com/journal15.html

"And then I do my best to destroy their mood: I bring bad news. Provoke a fight. Make a disparaging remark. Project a dire future. Sow uncertainty in the relationship. And when the other person is sour and sad, I feel relieved. It's back to normal. My mood improves dramatically and I try to cheer her up. Now if she does cheer up – it is REAL. It is my doing. I controlled it. And I controlled HER."

Excerpts from the Archives of the Narcissism List - Part 22 - Sam Vaknin
http://www.geocities.com/vaksam/archive22.html

"Narcissists – above absolutely everything else – are control freaks. To the narcissist, lack of control is excruciating pain."

Excerpts from the Archives of the Narcissism List - Part 22 - Sam Vaknin
http://www.geocities.com/vaksam/archive22.html

"This is why I dazzle them with my intellect and charm and wit and knowledge, with unprecedented intrusive interest in their petty, boring, housewifish lives – and then I let go abruptly. At this stage, they are so brittle, so vulnerable that they crash to a million shreds with the crystalline sound of agony."

Excerpts from the Archives of the Narcissism List - Part 27 - Sam Vaknin
http://www.geocities.com/vaksam/archive27.html

"The narcissist – wittingly or not – utilises people to buttress his self-image and self-worth. As long and as much as they are instrumental in achieving these goals – he holds them in high regard, they are valuable to him. He sees them only through this lens. This is a result of his inability to love humans: he lacks empathy, he thinks utility, and he reduces others to mere instruments. If they cease to 'function', if – no matter how inadvertently – they cause him to doubt this illusory, half-baked, self-esteem – they become the subject of a reign of terror. The narcissist then proceeds to hurt these 'insubordinate wretches'. He belittles and humiliates them. He displays aggression and violence in myriad forms. His behaviour metamorphosises kaleidoscopically, from over-valuation of the useful other to a severe devaluation of same."

The Soul of the Narcissist - Sam Vaknin
http://samvak.tripod.com/msla.html

"The personality disordered explodes in rage – because he implodes AND reacts to outside stimuli, simultaneously. Because he is a slave to magical thinking and, therefore, regards himself as omnipotent, omniscient and protected from the consequences of his own acts (immune) – the personality disordered often acts in a self-destructive and self-defeating manner. The similarities are so numerous and so striking that it seems safe to say that the personality disordered is in a constant state of acute anger."

Anger - The Common Sources of Personality Disorders - Sam Vaknin
http://samvak.tripod.com/mask.html

"Most personality disordered people are prone to be angry. Their anger is always sudden, raging, frightening and without an apparent provocation by an outside agent. It would seem that people suffering from personality disorders are in a CONSTANT state of anger, which is effectively suppressed most of the time. It manifests itself only when the person's defences are down, incapacitated, or adversely affected by circumstances, inner or external."

Anger - The Common Sources of Personality Disorders - Sam Vaknin
http://samvak.tripod.com/mask.html

"The personality disordered are afraid to show that they are angry to meaningful others because they are afraid to lose them. The borderline personality disordered is terrified of being abandoned, the narcissist (NPD) needs his Narcissistic Supply Sources, the paranoid – his persecutors and so on. These people prefer to direct their anger at people who are meaningless to them, people whose withdrawal will not constitute a threat to their precariously balanced personality. They yell at a waitress, berate a taxi driver, or explode at an underling."

Anger - The Common Sources of Personality Disorders - Sam Vaknin
http://samvak.tripod.com/mask.html

"Fiercely competitive in his demand for approval and acclaim, he distrusts competition because he associates it unconsciously with an unbridled urge to destroy. Hence he repudiates the competitive ideologies that flourished at an earlier stage of capitalist development and distrusts even their limited expression in sports and games. He extols cooperation and teamwork while harbouring deeply antisocial impulses. He praises respect for rules and regulations in the secret belief that they do not apply to himself. Acquisitive in the sense that his cravings have no limits, he does not accumulate goods and provisions against the future, in the manner of the acquisitive individualist of nineteenth-century political economy, but demands immediate gratification and lives in a state of restless, perpetually unsatisfied desire."

The Cultural Narcissist - Sam Vaknin
http://samvak.tripod.com/lasch.html

"Tell him that you would not like to ever see him again OR hear from him again and that - if he promises to let go - you promise to let go and forget the whole thing. Needless to say that if he does stalk you - you should contact the Police. Regarding the money: I don't know how much he owes you but whatever it is, it is a small price to pay for getting rid of a narcissist. You learned a lesson and you paid a tuition fee. This is the way of the world."

Excerpts from the Archives of the Narcissism List - Part 19 - Sam Vaknin
http://samvak.tripod.com/archive19.html

"I, for instance, firmly 'believe' that women are evil predators, out to suck my lifeblood and abandon me. So, I try and make them fulfil the prophecy. I try and make sure that they behave exactly in this manner, that they do not abnegate and ruin the model that I so craftily, so elaborately and so studiously designed. I tease them and betray them and bad mouth them and taunt them and torment them and stalk them and haunt them and pursue them and subjugate them and frustrate them until they do abandon me."

> Excerpts from the Archives of the Narcissism List - Part 19 - Sam Vaknin
> http://samvak.tripod.com/archive19.html

"Administer a modicum of narcissistic treatment (including verbal abuse) to the narcissist - and he/she is likely to vanish in a puff of indignant smoke. Narcissists shrivel, wither and die without Narcissistic Supply. Humiliation, disagreement, criticism, comparison with others, mirroring the narcissist's behaviour - are all great ways of getting rid of narcissists."

> Excerpts from the Archives of the Narcissism List - Part 1 - Sam Vaknin
> http://samvak.tripod.com/archive1.html

"I believe in the possibility of loving narcissists if one accepts them unconditionally, in a disillusioned and expectation-free manner. Narcissists are narcissists. This is what they are. Take them or leave them. Some of them are lovable. Most of them are highly charming and intelligent. The source of the misery of the victims of the narcissist is their disappointment, their disillusionment, their abrupt and tearing and tearful realisation that they fell in love with an ideal of their own invention, a phantasm, an illusion, a fata morgana. This 'waking up' is traumatic. The narcissist is forever the same. It is the victim who changes."

> Excerpts from the Archives of the Narcissism List - Part 1 - Sam Vaknin
> http://samvak.tripod.com/archive1.html

"I, personally, always inform and warn other people that I am a narcissist. Yet it never seemed to have dissuaded even one fervent lady from pursuing me (or, rather, my False Self). It did not deter one businessman from doing business with me. Frankly, it did not deter you from joining my list. Why is this? Because, having been forewarned, perhaps you stand to benefit without suffering. And, most probably, you do. But perhaps it is the irresistible attraction we all have to the 'other', the 'different' and, as a result, the 'risky'."

> Excerpts from the Archives of the Narcissism List - Part 1 - Sam Vaknin
> http://samvak.tripod.com/archive1.html

"The figures seem to indicate that a minimum of 1% (probably 3% and perhaps up to 5%) of the population above the age of 10 are narcissists. Now, factor in the parents, spouses, colleagues, friends, children, the children's families... This is the biggest under-diagnosed mental health pathology ever. Many researchers also believe that all Cluster B personality disorders (Histrionic, Antisocial, and Borderline) have a underlying foundation of pathological narcissism. This is getting close to 10% of the adult population. Staggering numbers."

Excerpts from the Archives of the Narcissism List - Part 1 - Sam Vaknin
http://samvak.tripod.com/archive1.html

"They interpret everything - even the most innocuous, inadvertent, and innocent - as designed to provoke and humiliate them. They sow fear, revulsion, hate, and malignant envy. They flail against the windmills of reality - a pathetic, forlorn, sight. But often they cause real and lasting damage - fortunately, mainly to themselves."

The Delusional Way Out - Sam Vaknin
http://samvak.tripod.com/journal42.html

"The narcissist's natural affinity with the criminal - his lack of empathy and compassion, his deficient social skills, his disregard for social laws and morals - now erupts and blossoms. He becomes a full fledged antisocial (sociopath or psychopath). He ignores the wishes and needs of others, he breaks the law, he violates all rights - natural and legal, he hold people in contempt and disdain, he derides society and its codes, he punishes the ignorant ingrates - that, to his mind, drove him to this state - by acting criminally and by jeopardising their safety, lives, or property."

The Delusional Way Out - Sam Vaknin
http://samvak.tripod.com/journal42.html

"The status of professional victim sits well with the partner's tendency to punish his self, namely: with his masochistic streak. The torment, which is a life with a Narcissist is a just punitive measure."

The Spouse / Mate / Partner of the Narcissist - Sam Vaknin
http://samvak.tripod.com/faq6.html

"Narcissists should be held accountable for most of what they do because they can tell wrong from right AND they can refrain from taking the actions they do take. They simply don't care enough about others to put to good use these twin abilities. A narcissist can be held responsible for some of his actions because he can tell right from wrong and can control most of his actions. He simply doesn't care to do so. Others are not important enough to him."

Excerpts from the Archives of the Narcissism List - Part 5 - Sam Vaknin
http://samvak.tripod.com/archive05.html

"I hate children. I hate them for being me."

Beware the Children - Sam Vaknin
http://samvak.tripod.com/journal36.html

"The Psychopath and the Narcissist
The psychopath (the Antisocial Personality Disorder) feels no remorse. The narcissist feels blame and guilt but then he instantly shifts them to others (MAINLY and OFTEN to his victim)."

Excerpts from the Archives of the Narcissism List - Part 34 - Sam Vaknin
http://samvak.tripod.com/archive34.html

"Devoid of the diversity of alternatives available to men – the narcissistic woman fights to maintain her most reliable Source of Supply: her children. Through insidious indoctrination, guilt formation, emotional sanctions, deprivation and other psychological mechanisms, she tries to induce in them a dependence, which cannot be easily unravelled."

Gender and the Narcissist - Sam Vaknin
http://samvak.tripod.com/faq34.html

"When he idealises you and you remain unmoved – you are frustrating and ingrate. When he devalues you and you ignore him – you are obstinate and deserving of even worse punishment. In short: you are infuriating because you won't be controlled."

Excerpts from the Archives of the Narcissism List - Part 34 - Sam Vaknin
http://samvak.tripod.com/archive34.html

"The role of 'professional victims' – ones whose existence and very identity is defined solely and entirely by their victimhood – is well researched in victimology. It doesn't make for a nice reading. These victim 'pros' are often more cruel, vengeful, vitriolic, discompassionate and violent than their abuser. They make a career of it. They identify with this role to the exclusion of all else. It is a danger to be avoided. And this is precisely what I called Narcissistic Contagion or Narcissism by Proxy."

Excerpts from the Archives of the Narcissism List - Part 34 - Sam Vaknin
http://samvak.tripod.com/archive34.html

"To react emotionally to a narcissist is like talking atheism to an Afghan fundamentalist. Narcissists have emotions, very strong ones, so terrifyingly strong and negative that they hide them, repress, block, and transmute them. They employ a myriad of defence mechanisms: Projective Identification, splitting, projection, intellectualisation, rationalisation... Any effort to emotionally relate to a narcissist is doomed to failure, alienation and rage."

Excerpts from the Archives of the Narcissism List - Part 2 - Sam Vaknin
http://samvak.tripod.com/archive02.html

"The narcissist is prone to magical thinking. He thinks about himself in terms of 'being chosen' or of 'having a destiny'. He believes that he has a 'direct line' to God, even, perversely, that God 'serves' him in certain junctions and conjunctures of his life, through divine intervention. He believes that his life is of such momentous importance, that it is micro-managed by God. The narcissist likes to play God to his human environment. In short, narcissism and religion go well together, because religion allows the narcissist to feel unique."

God, the Narcissist and Social Institutions - Sam Vaknin
http://samvak.tripod.com/faq47.html

"The narcissist elaborately stage manages his very being. His every movement, his tone of voice, his inflection, his poise, his text and subtext and context are carefully orchestrated to yield the maximum effect and to garner the most attention."

Conspicuous Existence - Sam Vaknin
http://samvak.tripod.com/journal38.html

"The narcissist does nothing and says nothing – or even thinks nothing – without first having computed the quantity of Narcissistic Supply his actions, utterances, or thoughts may yield. The visible narcissist is the tip of a gigantic, submerged, iceberg of seething reckoning. The narcissist is incessantly engaged in energy draining gauging of other people and their possible reactions to him. He estimates, he counts, he weighs and measures, he determines, evaluates, and enumerates, compares, despairs, and re-awakens. His fatigued brain is bathed with the drowning noise of stratagems and fears, rage and envy, anxiety and relief, addiction and rebellion, meditation and pre-meditation. The narcissist is a machine which never rests, not even in his dreams, and it has one purpose only – the securing and maximisation of Narcissistic Supply."

Conspicuous Existence - Sam Vaknin
http://samvak.tripod.com/journal38.html

"'Conspicuous existence' malignantly replaces 'real existence'. The myriad, ambivalent, forms of life are supplanted by the single obsession-compulsion of being seen, being observed, being reflected, being by proxy, through the gaze of others. The narcissist ceases to exist when not in company. His being fades when not discerned. Yet, he is unable to return the favour. He is a captive, oblivious to everything but his preoccupation. Emptied from within, devoured by his urge, the narcissist blindly stumbles from one relationship to another, from one warm body to the next, forever in search of that elusive creature – himself."

Conspicuous Existence - Sam Vaknin
http://samvak.tripod.com/journal38.html

"Hate is the complement of fear and I like being feared. It imbues me with an intoxicating sensation of omnipotence. I am veritably inebriated by the looks of horror or repulsion on people's faces. They know that I am capable of anything."

I Love to be Hated - Sam Vaknin
http://samvak.tripod.com/journal8.html

"The blind rage that this induces in the targets of my vitriolic diatribes provokes in me a surge of satisfaction and inner tranquillity not obtainable by any other means."

         I Love to be Hated - Sam Vaknin
         http://samvak.tripod.com/journal8.html

"It is my horrid future and inescapable punishment that carries the irresistible appeal. Like some strain of alien virus, it infects my better judgement and I succumb. In general, my weapon is the truth and human propensity to avoid it. In tactless breaching of every etiquette, I chastise and berate and snub and offer vitriolic opprobrium. A self-proclaimed Jeremiah, I hector and harangue from my many self-made pulpits."

         I Love to be Hated - Sam Vaknin
         http://samvak.tripod.com/journal8.html

"I am ruthless and devoid of scruples, capricious and unfathomable, emotion-less and asexual, omniscient, omnipotent and omni-present, a plague, a devastation, an inescapable verdict. I nurture my ill-repute, stoking it and fanning the flames of gossip. It is an enduring asset. Hate and fear are sure generators of attention. It is all about Narcissistic Supply."

         I Love to be Hated - Sam Vaknin
         http://samvak.tripod.com/journal8.html

"Narcissists are "evil" in an absent-minded, indifferent manner. It is not that they occupy Transylvanian castles, or plot to gorge on the blood of the innocent. They wound and hurt as a by-product of their firm belief that they are unique, that they deserve more and better, that they should not be subjected to other people's laws and should not be consumed by the mundane. Others to them are mere pawns, tools in the cosmically significant chessboard of their lives. In other words: dispensable."

  Excerpts from the Archives of the Narcissism List - Part 6 - Sam Vaknin
         http://samvak.tripod.com/archive06.html

"The narcissist inflicts pain and abuse on others. He devalues Sources of Supply, callously and offhandedly abandons them, and discards people, places, partnerships, and friendships unhesitatingly. Sudden shifts between sadism and altruism, abuse and 'love', ignoring and caring, abandoning and clinging, viciousness and remorse, the harsh and the tender – are, perhaps, the most difficult to comprehend and to accept. These swings produce in people around the narcissist emotional insecurity, an eroded sense of self-worth, fear, stress, and anxiety ('walking on eggshells'). Gradually, emotional paralysis ensues and they come to occupy the same emotional wasteland inhabited by the narcissist, his prisoners and hostages in more ways than one – and even when he is long out of their life."

Other People's Pain - Sam Vaknin
http://samvak.tripod.com/journal33.html

"False modesty is only one of a series of false behaviour patterns. The narcissist is a pathological liar, either implicitly or explicitly. His whole existence is a derivative of a False Self, a deceitful invention and its reflections. With false modesty he seeks to implicate others in his mind games, to co-opt them, to force them to collaborate while making ultimate use of social conventions of conduct. The narcissist, above all, is a shrewd manipulator of human character and its fault lines. He will never admit to this."

False Modesty - Sam Vaknin
http://samvak.tripod.com/faq36.html

"As time passes, the narcissist accumulates a mountain of mishaps, conflicts unresolved, pains well hidden, abrupt separations and bitter disappointments. He is subjected to a constant barrage of social criticism and condemnation."

Warped Reality and Retroactive Emotional Content - Sam Vaknin
http://samvak.tripod.com/faq39.html

"FIVE DON'T DO'S - How to Avoid the Wrath of the Narcissist. The TEN DO'S - How to Make Your Narcissist Dependent on You if You INSIST on Staying with Him."

Narcissistic Personality Disorder Tips - Sam Vaknin
http://samvak.tripod.com/npdtips.html

"What is the difference between NPD and BPD (Borderline Personality Disorder), OCD (Obsessive-Compulsive Disorder), AsPD (Antisocial PD), and other mental health disorders?"

>Narcissistic Personality Disorder and Other Mental Health Disorders
>- Sam Vaknin
>http://samvak.tripod.com/faq82.html

"The important differences between narcissism and the Antisocial Personality Disorder (AsPD or psychopaths, in the old terminology) are:
1. Inability or unwillingness to control impulses (AsPD);
2. Enhanced lack of empathy on the part of the AsPD;
3. Inability to form relationships with other humans, not even the narcissistically twisted types of relationships;
4. Total disregard for society, its conventions, social cues and social treaties.

As opposed to what Scott Peck says, narcissists are not evil - they lack the intention to cause harm. They are simply indifferent, callous and careless in their conduct and in their treatment of their fellow humans."

>Narcissistic Personality Disorder and Other Mental Health Disorders
>- Sam Vaknin
>http://samvak.tripod.com/faq82.html

"The narcissist admits to a problem only when abandoned, destitute, and devastated. He feels that he doesn't want any more of this. He wants to change. And there often are signs that he IS changing. And then it fades. He reverts to old form. The 'progress' he made evaporates virtually overnight. Many narcissists report the same process of progression followed by recidivist remission and many therapists refuse to treat narcissists because of the Sisyphean frustration involved."

>Self-Awareness and Healing - Sam Vaknin
>http://samvak.tripod.com/2.html

"The narcissist simply discards people when he becomes convinced that they can no longer provide him with Narcissistic Supply. This evaluation, subjective and highly emotionally charged, does not have to be grounded in reality. Suddenly - because of boredom, disagreement, disillusion, a fight, an act, inaction, or a mood - the narcissist wildly swings from idealisation to devaluation. He then 'disconnects' immediately. He needs all the energy that he can muster to obtain new Sources of Narcissistic Supply and would rather not spend these scarce and expensive resources over what he regards as human refuse, the waste left by the process of extraction of Narcissistic Supply."

The Narcissist as Sadist - Sam Vaknin
http://samvak.tripod.com/faq56.html

"A narcissist would tend to display the sadistic aspect of his personality in one of two cases:
1. That the very acts of sadism would generate Narcissistic Supply to be consumed by the narcissist ("I inflict pain, therefore I am superior") or
2. That the victims of his sadism are still his only or major Sources of Narcissistic Supply but are perceived by him to be intentionally frustrating and withholding it. Sadistic acts are his way of punishing them for not being docile, obedient, admiring and adoring as he expects them to be in view of his uniqueness, cosmic significance and special entitlement."

The Narcissist as Sadist - Sam Vaknin
http://samvak.tripod.com/faq56.html

"Sadists are often also masochists. In sadistic narcissists, there is, actually, a burning desire – nay, NEED – to be punished. In the grotesque mind of the narcissist, his punishment is equally his vindication. By being permanently on trial, the narcissist claims the high moral ground and the position of the martyr: misunderstood, discriminated against, unjustly roughed, outcast due to his very towering genius or other outstanding qualities. To conform to the cultural stereotype of the 'tormented artist' – the narcissist provokes his own suffering. He is thus validated. His grandiose fantasies acquire a modicum of substance. 'If I were not so special – they wouldn't have persecuted me so'. The persecution of the narcissist IS his uniqueness. He must be different, for better or for worse."

The Narcissist as Sadist - Sam Vaknin
http://samvak.tripod.com/faq56.html

"The narcissist is an artist of pain as much as any sadist. The difference between them is in their motivation. The narcissist tortures and abuses as a means to punish and to reassert superiority and grandiosity. The sadist does so for pure (usually, sexual) enjoyment. But both are adept at finding the chinks in people's armours. Both are ruthless and venomous in the pursuit of their prey. Both are unable to empathise with their victims, self-centred, and rigid. The narcissist abuses his victim verbally, mentally, or physically (often, in all three ways). He infiltrates her defences, shatters her self-confidence, confuses and confounds her, demeans and debases her. He invades her territory, abuses her confidence, exhausts her resources, hurts her loved ones, threatens her stability and security, involves her in his paranoid states of mind, frightens her out of her wits, withholds love and sex from her, prevents satisfaction and causes frustration, humiliates and insults her privately and in public, points out her shortcomings, criticises her profusely."

The Narcissist as Sadist - Sam Vaknin
http://samvak.tripod.com/faq56.html

"Very often, the narcissist acts sadistically in the guise of an enlightened interest in the welfare of his victim. He plays the psychiatrist to her psychopathology (totally dreamt up by him). He acts the guru to her need of guidance, the avuncular or father figure, the teacher, the only true friend, the old and the experienced. All this in order to weaken her defences and to lay siege to her disintegrating nerves. So subtle and poisonous is the narcissistic variant of sadism that it might well be regarded as the most dangerous of all."

The Narcissist as Sadist - Sam Vaknin
http://samvak.tripod.com/faq56.html

"To the narcissist, other humans are mere instruments, Sources of Narcissistic Supply. He sees no reason to dedicate thought to their needs, wishes, wants, desires and fears. He derails their life with ease and benevolent ignorance."

The Narcissist's Victims - Sam Vaknin
http://samvak.tripod.com/faq38.html

"Sooner, or later, everyone around the narcissist is bound to become his victim. People are sucked - voluntarily or involuntarily - into the turbulence that constitutes his life, into the black hole that is his personality, into the whirlwind, which makes up his interpersonal relationships. Different people are hurt by different aspects of the narcissist's life and psychological makeup. Some trust him and rely on him, only to be bitterly disappointed. Others love him and discover that he cannot reciprocate. Yet others are forced to live vicariously, through him."

The Narcissist's Victims - Sam Vaknin
http://samvak.tripod.com/faq38.html

"The narcissist exudes the air of someone really capable of loving or of being hurt, of one passionate and soft, empathic and caring. Most people are misled into believing that he is even more human than usual. They fall in love with the mirage, the fleeting image, with the fata morgana of a lush emotional oasis in the midst of their emotional desert. They succumb to the luring proposition. They give in, give up, and give everything only to be discarded ruthlessly when judged by the narcissist to be no longer useful."

The Narcissist's Victims - Sam Vaknin
http://samvak.tripod.com/faq38.html

"Riding high on the crest of the narcissist's over-valuation only to crash into the abysmal depths of his devaluation, they lose control over their emotional life. The narcissist drains them, exhausts their resources, sucks the blood-life of Narcissistic Supply from their dwindling, depleted selves. This emotional roller coaster is so harrowing that the experience borders on the truly traumatic."

The Narcissist's Victims - Sam Vaknin
http://samvak.tripod.com/faq38.html

"The narcissist's employer, for instance, is misled by his apparent seriousness, industriousness, ambition, willing to sacrifice, honesty, thoroughness and a host of other utterly fake qualities. They are fake because they are directed at securing Narcissistic Supply rather than at doing a good job. His clients and suppliers may suffer from the same illusion. And his false emanations are not restricted to messages with emotional content. They may contain wrong or false or partial information. The narcissist does not hesitate to lie, deceive, or 'expose' (misleading) half-truths. He appears to be so intelligent, so charming and, therefore, so reliable – that he tends out among the crooks, con (short for confidence)-men and villains. He is a convincing conjurer of words, signs, behaviours, and body language."

The Narcissist's Victims - Sam Vaknin
http://samvak.tripod.com/faq38.html

"He attacks those he thinks take him for granted, or those who fail to recognise his grandiosity. And they, alas, include just about everyone he knows."

The Narcissist's Victims - Sam Vaknin
http://samvak.tripod.com/faq38.html

"Is pathological narcissism the outcome of inherited traits – or the sad result of abusive and traumatising upbringing? Or, maybe it is the confluence of both? It is a common occurrence, after all, that, in the same family, with the same set of parents and an identical emotional environment – some siblings grow to be malignant narcissists, while others are perfectly 'normal'. Surely, this indicates a predisposition of some people to developing narcissism, a part of one's genetic heritage. This vigorous debate may be the offshoot of obfuscating semantics."

The Selfish Gene - The Genetic Underpinnings of Narcissism
- Sam Vaknin
http://samvak.tripod.com/journal43.html

"An array of coordinated genes is required to explain even the minutest human phenomenon. 'Discoveries' of a 'gambling gene' here and an 'aggression gene' there are derided by the more serious and less publicity-prone scholars. Yet, it would seem that even complex behaviours such as risk taking, reckless driving, and compulsive shopping have genetic underpinnings."

The Selfish Gene - The Genetic Underpinnings of Narcissism
- Sam Vaknin
http://samvak.tripod.com/journal43.html

"The narcissist fakes feelings and their outer expression in order to impress others, to gain their sympathy or to motivate them to act in a manner benefiting the narcissist and promoting his interests."

The Inappropriate Affect - Sam Vaknin
http://samvak.tripod.com/faq41.html

"He is barren, devoid of any inkling of true feeling, even mocking. He looks down upon those who succumb to the weakness of experiencing emotions and holds them in contempt. He berates and debases them. This is the heartless mechanism of Simulated Affect. This mechanism lies at the core of the narcissist's inability to empathise with his fellow human beings."

The Inappropriate Affect - Sam Vaknin
http://samvak.tripod.com/faq41.html

"Question: How to recognise a narcissist before it is 'too late'?"

How to Recognise a Narcissist? - Sam Vaknin
http://samvak.tripod.com/faq58.html

"People suffering from the full blown, all-pervasive, personality distorting mental health disorder known as the Narcissistic Personality Disorder (NPD) - are, indeed, more prone to violence than others. Actually, the differential diagnosis (the difference) between NPD and AsPD (Antisocial PD, psychopaths) is very blurred."

Can the Narcissist Become Violent? - Sam Vaknin
http://samvak.tripod.com/9.html

"Most psychopaths have narcissistic traits and many a narcissist are also sadists. Both types are devoid of empathy, remorseless, ruthless, and relentless in their pursuit of their goals (the narcissist's goal is Narcissistic Supply or the avoidance of narcissistic injury). Narcissists often use verbal and psychological abuse and violence against those closest to them."

Can the Narcissist Become Violent? - Sam Vaknin
http://samvak.tripod.com/9.html

"He does not require – nor does he seek – his parents' or his siblings' love, or to be loved by his children. He casts them as the audience in the theatre of his inflated grandiosity. He wishes to impress them, shock them, threaten them, infuse them with awe, inspire them, attract their attention, subjugate them, or manipulate them. He emulates and simulates an entire range of emotions and employs every means to achieve these effects. He lies (narcissists are pathological liars – their very self is a false one). He plays the pitiful, or, its opposite, the resilient and reliable. He stuns and shines with outstanding intellectual, or physical (or anything else appreciated by the members of the family) capacities and achievements."

The Narcissist and His Family - Sam Vaknin
http://samvak.tripod.com/faq22.html

"As they mature, they often refuse to continue to play the mindless pawns in his chess game. They hold grudges against him for what he has done to them in the past, when they were less capable of resistance. They can gauge his true stature, talents and achievements – which, usually, lag far behind the claims that he makes."

The Narcissist and His Family - Sam Vaknin
http://samvak.tripod.com/faq22.html

"A parent diagnosed with full-fledged Narcissistic Personality Disorder (NPD) should be denied custody and be granted only restricted rights of visitation under supervision."

The Narcissist and His Family - Sam Vaknin
http://samvak.tripod.com/faq22.html

"The narcissist begins to see their potential to be edifying, reliable and satisfactory Sources of Narcissistic Supply. His attitude, then, is completely transformed. The former threats have now become promising potentials. He cultivates those whom he trusts to be the most rewarding. He encourages them to idolise him, to adore him, to be awed by him, to admire his deeds and capabilities, to learn to blindly trust and obey him, in short to surrender to his charisma and to become submerged in his folies-de-grandeur."

The Narcissist and His Family - Sam Vaknin
http://samvak.tripod.com/faq22.html

"I hate holidays and birthdays, including my birthday. It is because I hate it when other people are happy if I am not the cause of it. I have to be the prime mover and shaker of EVERYONE's moods. And no one will tell me HOW I should feel. I am my own master. I feel that their happiness is false, fake, forced. I feel that they are hypocrites, dissimulating joy where there is none. I feel envious, humiliated by my envy, and enraged by my humiliation. I feel that they are the recipients of a gift I will never have: the ability to enjoy life and to feel joy. And then I do my best to destroy their mood. I bring bad news."

A Holiday Grudge - Sam Vaknin
http://samvak.tripod.com/journal40.html

"When I have money, I can exercise my sadistic urges freely and with little fear of repercussions."

The Silver Pieces of the Narcissist - Sam Vaknin
http://samvak.tripod.com/journal44.html

"No, I do not crave money, nor care for it. I need the power that it bestows on me to dare, to flare, to conquer, to oppose, to resist, to taunt, and to torment."

The Silver Pieces of the Narcissist - Sam Vaknin
http://samvak.tripod.com/journal44.html

"To subjugate another, one must be capricious, unscrupulous, ruthless, obsessive, hateful, vindictive, and penetrating. One must spot the cracks of vulnerability, the crumbling foundations of susceptibility, the pains, the trigger mechanisms, the Pavlovian reactions of hate, and fear, and hope, and anger. Money liberates my mind."

The Silver Pieces of the Narcissist - Sam Vaknin
http://samvak.tripod.com/journal44.html

"When impoverished, I am altruism embodied – the best of friends, the most caring of tutors, a benevolent guide, a lover of humanity, and a fierce fighter against narcissism, sadism, and abuse in all their myriad forms. I adhere, I obey, I succumb, I agree wholeheartedly, I praise, condone, idolise, and applaud. I am the perfect audience, an admirer and an adulator, a worm and an amoeba – spineless, adaptable in form, slithery flexibility itself. To behave so is unbearable for a narcissist, hence my addiction to money (really, to freedom) in all its forms. It is my evolutionary ladder from slime to the sublime – to mastery."

The Silver Pieces of the Narcissist - Sam Vaknin
http://samvak.tripod.com/journal44.html

"The narcissist may study a given subject diligently and in great depth in order to impress people later with this newly acquired erudition. But, having served its purpose, the narcissist lets the knowledge thus acquired evaporate."

The Unstable Narcissist - Sam Vaknin
http://samvak.tripod.com/faq32.html

"Another – even more common – case is the 'career narcissist'. This narcissist marries, divorces and remarries with dizzying speed. Everything in his life is in constant flux: friends, emotions, judgements, values, beliefs, place of residence, affiliations, hobbies. Everything, that is, except his work."

The Unstable Narcissist - Sam Vaknin
http://samvak.tripod.com/faq32.html

"He perseveres in one workplace or one job, patiently, persistently and blindly climbing up the ladder or treading the career path. In his pursuit of job fulfilment and achievements, the narcissist is ruthless and unscrupulous – and, very often, successful."

The Unstable Narcissist - Sam Vaknin
http://samvak.tripod.com/faq32.html

"If you wish to stay out of her life altogether – why would you care what she does with her life? I know it's a cruel sentence. But there is no half separation as there is no half pregnancy. To say goodbye to another person is easy."

Excerpts from the Archives of the Narcissism List - Part 31 - Sam Vaknin

http://samvak.tripod.com/archive31.html

"Deploying money to control others IS narcissistic. The narcissist tries to make significant others financially dependent on him by preventing them from obtaining a job, keeping a bank account, or having access to money. Some narcissists secure this dependence by threatening and being verbally or physically abusive to the other – or by berating the partner and eroding her self-esteem to the point where she is afraid or ashamed to look for a job or to otherwise financially fend for herself."

Excerpts from the Archives of the Narcissism List - Part 31 - Sam Vaknin
http://samvak.tripod.com/archive31.html

"Some narcissists are impulsive – others are control freaks. The important thing is the use of money as a tool of subjugation of others."

Excerpts from the Archives of the Narcissism List - Part 31 - Sam Vaknin
http://samvak.tripod.com/archive31.html

"I just meant to distinguish between those victims who don't know better and get burnt – and those who KNOWINGLY, WILLINGLY, sometimes for the fun of it (risk/adventure), sometimes due to vanity (I will be the one to break him or to save him) – go near narcissists. The first class of victims are real victims. But I refuse to accept victimology. I think it is degrading and scientifically wrong to assume – as a working hypothesis – that victims WANT to be victimised."

Excerpts from the Archives of the Narcissism List - Part 8 - Sam Vaknin
http://samvak.tripod.com/archive08.html

"Question: Why does he keep coming back? I keep dumping my narcissist – and he keeps coming back for more. I accept him (can't resist him when he is his charming self). But then things go awry and the cycle repeats itself. Why does he keep coming back?

Answer: Your narcissist keeps coming back and remains fixated on you because he has no free libido to employ in the pursuit of alternative sources. And because you keep accepting him back."

Why Does He Keep Coming Back? - Sam Vaknin
http://samvak.tripod.com/3.html

"Being the victim of a narcissist is a condition no less pernicious than being a narcissist. Great efforts are required to leave a narcissist and physical separation is only the first step. One can abandon a narcissist – but the narcissist is slow to abandon its victims. It is there, lurking, rendering existence unreal, twisting and distorting with no respite, an inner, remorseless voice, lacking in compassion and empathy for its victim. And the narcissist is there spiritually long after it has vanished physically."

Excerpts from the Archives of the Narcissism List - Part 6 - Sam Vaknin
http://samvak.tripod.com/archive06.html

"It is true that he is a chauvinistic narcissist with repulsive behaviours. But all he needs is a little love and he will be straightened out. I will rescue him from his misery and misfortune. I will give him the love that he lacked as a kid. Then his narcissism will vanish and we will live happily ever after."

Excerpts from the Archives of the Narcissism List - Part 1 - Sam Vaknin
http://samvak.tripod.com/archive1.html

"Gradually, the narcissist distorts the personalities of those he is in constant touch with, casts them in his defective mould, limits them, redirects them, and inhibits them. When sufficiently cloned, the narcissist uses the effected personalities as narcissistic proxies, narcissistic vehicles of vicarious narcissism."

Narcissism by Proxy - Sam Vaknin
http://samvak.tripod.com/faq42.html

"Often, these behaviours, acts and emotions induced by the proximity to the narcissist – bring about harsh consequences to their perpetrators. These consequences need not necessarily be disastrous, but an emotional crisis can be as calamitous as a physical or material catastrophe. A catastrophe is bound to happen because the narcissist's prey is not equipped to deal with the crises that are the narcissist's daily bread and which, now, are delegated and relegated to his proxy."

Narcissism by Proxy - Sam Vaknin
http://samvak.tripod.com/faq42.html

"Question: What is the mechanism behind the cycles of over-valuation and devaluation in the narcissist's life?
Answer: Cycles of over-valuation (idealisation) followed by devaluation characterise many personality disorders (they are even more typical of Borderline PD than of NPD, for example). They reflect the need to be secure, protected against the vicious and capricious whims of others, shielded from the hurt that they can inflict. Such a shield is constructed from the mercurial twin substances of idealisation and disillusionment."

Narcissistic Allocation - Sam Vaknin
http://samvak.tripod.com/faq44.html

"The narcissist now faces the daunting task of evaluating the potential content and extend of Narcissistic Supply of each and every one of the potential collaborators. He does so by rating each one of them. The stimulus with the highest rating is, naturally, selected. It offers 'the best value for money', the most cost efficient proposition. The narcissist immediately over-values and idealises it. This is the narcissistic equivalent of getting emotionally attached and of bonding."

Narcissistic Allocation - Sam Vaknin
http://samvak.tripod.com/faq44.html

"The narcissist knows how to charm, how to simulate emotions, how to flatter. Many narcissists are gifted actors, having acted the role of their False Self for so long. They wine the targeted Supply Source (whether Primary or Secondary) and dine it. They compliment and flatter, always present, forever interested. Their genuine and keen (though selfish) immersion in the other, their overt high regard for him or her (a result of the idealisation), their almost submissiveness - are alluring. It is nigh impossible to resist a narcissist on the prowl for Sources of Supply. At this stage, his energies are all focused and dedicated to the task."

Narcissistic Allocation - Sam Vaknin
http://samvak.tripod.com/faq44.html

"The more the narcissist convinces himself that his sources are perfect, grand, comprehensive, authoritative, omniscient, omnipotent, beautiful, powerful, rich and so on – the better he feels. The narcissist has to idealise his Supply Sources in order to value the supply that he derives from them. This leads to over-valuation and results in the formation of an unrealistic picture of others. The fall is inevitable. Disillusionment and disappointment ensue. The slightest criticism, disagreement, shades of opinion - are interpreted by the narcissist as an all out assault against his very existence. The previous appraisal is sharply reversed.

For example: the same people are judged stupid who were previously deemed to possess genius. This is the devaluation part of the cycle - and it is very painful both to the narcissist and to the devalued (for very different reasons, of course). The narcissist mourns the loss of a promising 'investment opportunity' (Source of Narcissistic Supply). Conversely, the 'investment opportunity' mourns the loss of the narcissist."

Narcissistic Allocation - Sam Vaknin
http://samvak.tripod.com/faq44.html

"The narcissist has no genuine emotions. He can be madly in 'love' with a woman (Secondary Narcissistic Supply Source) because she is famous/she has money/she admires him/she is a native and he is an immigrant/she comes from the right family/she is unique in a manner positively reflecting on the narcissist's perceived uniqueness/she remembers past successes of the narcissist. Yet, this 'love' disappears immediately when her usefulness runs its course or when a better 'qualified' Source of Supply presents herself."

Narcissistic Allocation - Sam Vaknin
http://samvak.tripod.com/faq44.html

"Moving on is a process, not a decision or an event. First, one has to acknowledge and accept reality. It is a volcanic, shattering, agonising series of little, nibbling, thoughts and strong, voluptuous resistances. Once the battle is won, and harsh and painful realities are assimilated, one can move on to the learning phase. We label. We assemble material. We gather knowledge. We compare experiences. We digest. We have insights. Then we decide and we act."

Surviving the Narcissist - Sam Vaknin
http://samvak.tripod.com/faq80.html

"Narcissists are terrified of being abandoned exactly as co-dependents and borderlines are. BUT their solution is different. Co-dependents cling. Borderlines are emotionally labile and react disastrously to the faintest hint of being abandoned. Narcissists FACILITATE the abandonment. They MAKE SURE that they are abandoned. This way they achieve two goals:
1. Getting it over with – The narcissist has a very low threshold of tolerance to uncertainty and inconvenience, emotional or material.
2. Narcissists are very impatient and 'spoiled'. They cannot delay gratification OR impending doom. They must have it all NOW, good or bad."

Surviving the Narcissist - Sam Vaknin
http://samvak.tripod.com/faq80.html

"Narcissists home in on potential suppliers like cruise missiles. They are excellent at imitating emotions, exhibiting the right timely behaviours and at manipulating."

Surviving the Narcissist - Sam Vaknin
http://samvak.tripod.com/faq80.html

"If the relationship with a narcissist is so rewarding, why are inverted narcissists so unhappy?"

Surviving the Narcissist - Sam Vaknin
http://samvak.tripod.com/faq80.html

"They are aware of what they are doing to others – but they do not care. Sometimes, they sadistically taunt and torment people – but they do not perceive this to be evil – merely amusing."

Surviving the Narcissist - Sam Vaknin
http://samvak.tripod.com/faq80.html

"Narcissists can be happily married to submissive, subservient, self-deprecating, echoing, mirroring and indiscriminately supportive spouses. They also do well with masochists. But it is difficult to imagine that a healthy, normal person would be happy in such a folie-a-deux ('madness in twosome')."

Surviving the Narcissist - Sam Vaknin
http://samvak.tripod.com/faq80.html

"BUT many a spouse/friend/mate/partner like to BELIEVE that - given sufficient time and patience - they will be the ones to release the narcissist from his wrenching bondage. They think that they can 'rescue' the narcissist, shield him from his (distorted) self, as it were. The narcissist makes use of this naiveté and exploits it to his benefit."

Surviving the Narcissist - Sam Vaknin
http://samvak.tripod.com/faq80.html

"Thus, perhaps we should invent "VoNPD", another mental health category - Victims of NPD. They experience shame and anger for their past helplessness and submissiveness. They are hurt and sensitised by the harrowing experience of sharing a simulated existence with a simulated person, the narcissist. They are scarred and often suffer from Post-Traumatic Stress Disorder (PTSD)."

Surviving the Narcissist - Sam Vaknin
http://samvak.tripod.com/faq80.html

"But can't we act civilised and remain on friendly terms with our narcissist ex? Never forget that narcissists (full fledged ones) are nice to others when:
  a. They want something - Narcissistic Supply, help, support, votes, money... They prepare the ground, manipulate you and then come out with the 'small favour' they need or ask you blatantly or surreptitiously for Narcissistic Supply ('What did you think about my performance...', 'Do you think that I really deserve the Nobel Prize?').
  b. They feel threatened and they want to neuter the threat by smothering it with oozing pleasantries.
  c. They have just been infused with an overdose of Narcissistic Supply and they feel magnanimous and magnificent and ideal and perfect. To show magnanimity is a way of flaunting one's impeccable divine credentials. It is an act of grandiosity. You are an irrelevant prop in this spectacle, a mere receptacle of the narcissist's overflowing, self-contented infatuation with his False Self."

Surviving the Narcissist - Sam Vaknin
http://samvak.tripod.com/faq80.html

"But there is nothing, which reminds the narcissist more of the totality of his envious experiences than happiness. Narcissists lash out at happy people out of their own deprivation."

Surviving the Narcissist - Sam Vaknin
http://samvak.tripod.com/faq80.html

"People around him are transformed by him and become timid or rebellious, paranoid or phobic, depressed or manic. They are reduced not only in the eyes of the narcissist - but in reality and in their own eyes - to functions, to objects. In their effort to satisfy the need of the narcissist to exist - they very often neglect their own existence. They feel that something is sick and wrong in their lives. But they are so entrapped, so much part of the narcissist's personal mythology that they cannot cut loose. Manipulated through guilt, leveraged through fear - they are but a shadow of their former selves. They have contracted the disease of narcissism. They have been infected and poisoned. They have been branded."

Narcissistic Branding and Narcissistic Contagion - Sam Vaknin
http://samvak.tripod.com/faq46.html

"Religious authority allows the narcissist to indulge his sadistic urges and to exercise his misogynism freely and openly. Such a narcissist is likely to taunt and torment his followers, hector and chastise them, humiliate and berate them, abuse them spiritually, or even sexually. The narcissist whose source of authority is religious is looking for obedient and unquestioning slaves upon whom to exercise his capricious and wicked mastery."

For the Love of God - Sam Vaknin
http://samvak.tripod.com/journal45.html

"Religious authority also secures the narcissist's Narcissistic Supply. His coreligionists, members of his congregation, his parish, his constituency, his audience - are transformed into loyal and stable Sources of Narcissistic Supply."

For the Love of God - Sam Vaknin
http://samvak.tripod.com/journal45.html

"Avoiding eye contact and evading conversation is the narcissist's haughty way of saying: 'I am above these people who are so undeserving of my company'. The narcissist - by avoiding other people who might contradict and shatter his or her grandiose fantasies - is actually employing a DEFENCE mechanism."

Excerpts from the Archives of the Narcissism List - Part 28 - Sam Vaknin
http://samvak.tripod.com/archive28.html

"In developing the narcissistic personality, it is important to consider the parental history. A highly critical family environment dominated by extremely demanding parents generally marks the childhood of the narcissistic character. In such a family the child's primary function is to enhance the mother's or father's self-esteem: the child as accessory. When the child in such a family fails to live up to such stringent parental expectations (which are inevitable), the child will be the target of criticism, either direct or indirect, and suffer rejection. The damage occurs during the child's formative years, a time when nurturing and the discovery and fostering of a functional personality are crucial."

Message #473 in the Narcissistic Abuse List - Sam Vaknin
http://groups.yahoo.com/group/narcissisticabuse/

"Question: How can you help someone who is with a narcissist and is not strong enough to leave?

Answer: It depends what is the source of the weakness. If it is objective - money matters, for instance - it is relatively easy to solve. But if the dependence is emotional, it is very difficult because the relationship with the narcissist caters to very deep-set, imprinted, emotional needs and landscape of the partner. The partner perceives the relationship as gratifying, colourful, fascinating, unique, promising. It is a combination of adrenaline-rush and Land of Oz fantasy. It is very difficult to beat. Only professional intervention can tackle real co-dependence. Having said that, the most important thing is to provide an emotional alternative by being a real friend: understanding, supportive, insightful, and non-addictive (i.e., do not encourage co-dependence on you instead of on the narcissist). It is a long, arduous process with uncertain outcomes."

Relationships with Abusive Narcissists Online Chat Transcript
http://healthyplace.com/communities/personality_disorders/site/Transcripts/abusive_narcissists.htm

"David: What, then, can the other person in this relationship expect from the narcissist?

Vaknin: The narcissist regards the 'significant other' as one would regard an instrument or implement. It is the Source of his Narcissistic Supply, his extension, a mirror, an echo chamber, the symbiont. In short, the narcissist is never complete without his spouse or mate."

Relationships with Abusive Narcissists Online Chat Transcript
http://healthyplace.com/communities/personality_disorders/site/Transcripts/abusive_narcissists.htm

"David: So, if you are the victim of the narcissist, what kind of life can you look forward to?

Vaknin: You will be required to deny your self – your hopes, your dreams, your fears, your aspirations, your sexual needs, your emotional needs, and sometimes your material needs. You will be asked to deny reality and ignore it. It is very disorientating. Most victims feel that they are going crazy or that they are guilty of something obscure, opaque, and ominous. It is Kafkaesque: an endless, on-going trial without clear laws, known procedures, and identified judges. It is nightmarish."

Relationships with Abusive Narcissists Online Chat Transcript
http://healthyplace.com/communities/personality_disorders/site/Transcripts/abusive_narcissists.htm

"David: What you're saying, Sam, is that to get rid of the abusive or vindictive narcissist, a simple 'no' or 'our relationship is over' is usually not enough.

Vaknin: No, it is not enough. The vindictive narcissist must eliminate the source of his frustration either by subsuming it (re-establishing the relationship) or by punishing and humiliating it and thus establishing an imaginary symmetry and restoring the narcissist's sense of omnipotence. Vindictive narcissists are addicted to power and fear as Sources of Narcissistic Supply. Unstable ('normal') narcissists are addicted to attention and their Sources of Supply are interchangeable."

Relationships with Abusive Narcissists Online Chat Transcript
http://healthyplace.com/communities/personality_disorders/site/Transcripts/abusive_narcissists.htm

"David: Are the behaviours exhibited by females the same or similar to those of male narcissists?

Vaknin: Largely, yes. The behaviours are identical – the targets are different. Women narcissists will tend to abuse 'outside the family' (neighbours, friends, colleagues, employees). Male narcissists tend to abuse 'inside the family' (mainly their spouse) and at work. But this is a very weak distinction. Narcissism is such an all-pervasive personality disorder that it characterises the narcissist more than his gender, race, ethnic affiliation, socio-economic stratum, sexual orientation, or any other single determinant does."

Relationships with Abusive Narcissists Online Chat Transcript
http://healthyplace.com/communities/personality_disorders/site/Transcripts/abusive_narcissists.htm

"Checky: Hi, Dr. Vaknin. You're up late! What is your opinion on this: Can an abusive narcissist ever become a tolerable narcissist while in a marriage and when the abuse has taken place over many years?

David: I'll add to that question: Can the narcissist ever make a 'real' change in his abusive behaviour or is this ingrained in his personality?

Vaknin: Whether the narcissist is tolerable or not is up to the spouse or partner to decide. If you are asking whether the narcissist can ameliorate, tone down, be mollified, reduce his intensity, refrain from abuse and modify his behaviour – sure, he can. It depends what is in it for him. Narcissists are the consummate and ultimate actors. They maintain emotional resonance tables. They monitor other people's reactions and behaviour – and they are mimetic (imitators). But it is not a real and profound change. It is merely behaviour modification and it is reversible. I hasten to say that certain schools of psychotherapy claim success in treating pathological narcissism, notably the Cognitive-Behavioural Therapies and psychodynamic therapies – as well as more exotic, Eastern, therapies."

Relationships with Abusive Narcissists Online Chat Transcript
http://healthyplace.com/communities/personality_disorders/site/Transcripts/abusive_narcissists.htm

"Question: Sam Vaknin, you know that you are a narcissist. Do most narcissists have the same self-realisation or do they think that something is wrong with everyone else but themselves?

Vaknin: Exceedingly few narcissists are self-aware. Actually, you might say that self-awareness is the antonym of narcissism. Most narcissists go through life convinced that something is wrong with everyone, that they are victimised, misunderstood, underestimated by intellectual midgets, abused (yes, abused!) by envious others and so on. In essence, the narcissist projects his own emotional barren and vitriolic landscape onto his environment. He sometimes forces people around him to behave in a way that justifies his expectations of them. This is called Projective Identification."

Relationships with Abusive Narcissists Online Chat Transcript
http://healthyplace.com/communities/personality_disorders/site/Transcripts/abusive_narcissists.htm

"Question: Does the narcissist have a conscience?

Vaknin: No. Conscience is predicated on empathy. One puts oneself in other people's 'shoes' and feels the way they do. Without empathy, there can be no love or conscience. Indeed, the narcissist has neither. To him, people are silhouettes, penumbral projections on the walls of his inflated sense of self, figments of his fantasies. How can one regret anything if one is a solipsist (i.e., recognises only his reality and no one else's)?"

Relationships with Abusive Narcissists Online Chat Transcript
http://healthyplace.com/communities/personality_disorders/site/Transcripts/abusive_narcissists.htm

"Question: You keep writing about male narcissists. Is there any difference between male narcissists and female narcissists?

Answer: The Narcissistic Personality Disorder (as opposed, for instance, to the Borderline or the Histrionic Personality Disorders, which afflict women more than men) seems to conform to social mores and to the prevailing ethos of capitalism. Social thinkers like Lasch speculated that modern American culture - a narcissistic, self-centred one - increases the rate of incidence of the Narcissistic Personality Disorder."

Gender and the Narcissist - Sam Vaknin
http://samvak.tripod.com/faq34.html

"There is always a locus of loss in the narcissist's life. He may be faithful to his wife and a model family man - but then he is likely to change jobs frequently and renege on his financial and social obligations. Or, he may be a brilliant achiever - scientist, doctor, CEO, actor, pastor, politician, journalist - with a steady, long-term and successful career - but a lousy homemaker, thrice divorced, unfaithful, unstable, always on the lookout for better Narcissistic Supply."

The Losses of the Narcissist - Sam Vaknin
http://samvak.tripod.com/journal49.html

"The narcissist cruises through his life as a tourist would through an exotic island. He observes events and people, his own experiences and loved ones - as a spectator would a movie that at times is mildly exciting and at others mildly boring. He is never fully there, entirely present, irreversibly committed. He is constantly with one hand on his emotional escape hatch, ready to bail out, to absent himself, to re-invent his life in another place, with other people. The narcissist is a coward, terrified of his True Self and protective of the deceit that is his new existence. He feels no pain. He feels no love. He feels no life."

The Losses of the Narcissist - Sam Vaknin
http://samvak.tripod.com/journal49.html

"The narcissist is aware of his propensity to lose everything that could have been of value, meaning, and significance in his life. If he is inclined to magical thinking and alloplastic defences, he blames life, or fate, or country, or his boss, or his nearest and dearest for his uninterrupted string of losses. Otherwise, he attributes it to people's inability to cope with his outstanding talents, towering intellect, or rare abilities. His losses, he convinces himself, are the outcomes of pettiness, pusillanimity, envy, malice, and ignorance. It would have turned out the same way even had he behaved differently, he consoles himself."

The Losses of the Narcissist - Sam Vaknin
http://samvak.tripod.com/journal49.html

"Losing my wife - with whom I spent nine years of my life - was devastating. I felt denuded and annulled. But once the divorce was over, I forgot about her completely. I deleted her memory so thoroughly that I very rarely think and never dream about her. I am never sad. I never stop to think 'what if', to derive lessons, to obtain closure. I am not pretending, nor am I putting effort into this selective amnesia. It happened serendipitously, like a valve shut tight. I feel proud of this ability of mine to un-be."

The Losses of the Narcissist - Sam Vaknin
http://samvak.tripod.com/journal49.html

"Narcissists are accustomed to loss. Their obnoxious personality and intolerable behaviours makes them lose friends and spouses, mates and colleagues, jobs and family. Their peripatetic nature, their constant mobility and instability causes them to lose everything else: their place of residence, their property, their businesses, their country, and their language."

The Losses of the Narcissist - Sam Vaknin
http://samvak.tripod.com/journal49.html

"The narcissist is seething with enmity and venom. He is a receptacle of unbridled hatred, animosity, and hostility. When he can, the narcissist often turns to physical violence. But the non-physical manifestations of his pent-up bile are even more terrifying, more all-pervasive, and more lasting. Beware of narcissists bearing gifts. They are bound to explode in your faces, or poison you. The narcissist hates you wholeheartedly and thoroughly simply because you are. Remembering this has a survival value."

Transformations of Aggression - Sam Vaknin
http://samvak.tripod.com/journal50.html

"Once the relationship is clinched and the victim is 'hooked' - the narcissist tries to minimise his contributions. He regards his input as a contractual maintenance chore and the unpleasant and inevitable price he has to pay for his Narcissistic Supply."

The Misanthropic Altruist - Sam Vaknin
http://www.narcissistic-abuse.com/journal81.html

"To a narcissist-employer, the members of his 'staff' are Secondary Sources of Narcissistic Supply. Their role is to accumulate the supply (in human speak, remember events that support the grandiose self-image of the narcissist) and to regulate the Narcissistic Supply of the narcissist during dry spells (simply put, to adulate, adore, admire, agree, provide attention and approval and so on or, in other words, be an audience). The staff (or should we say 'stuff'?) is supposed to remain passive. The narcissist is not interested in anything but the simplest function of mirroring. When the mirror acquires a personality and a life of its own, the narcissist is incensed. When independent minded, an employee might be in danger of being sacked by his employer (an act which demonstrates the employer's omnipotence)."

The Narcissist in the Workplace - Sam Vaknin
http://samvak.tripod.com/faq81.html

"Vielen: When a narcissist abandons someone, can he erase them totally out of his memory? And does he want to?

Vaknin: Yes, I did that with my ex-wife. Actually, there are two typical reactions:

One is, to totally erase and delete every shred of a remnant of a shadow of a memory of her and the common life (the more common reaction), or as vindictive narcissists do - to stalk, pursue, invade, control, threaten and manipulate the ex."

Relationships with Abusive Narcissists Online Chat Transcript
http://healthyplace.com/communities/personality_disorders/site/Transcripts/abusive_narcissists.htm

"David: Is there a common characteristic, common personality trait, among the victims of narcissists?

Vaknin: Yes, their submissiveness and eagerness to please. This is because the narcissist becomes their drug, their addiction. Without him, it is a world of black and white. With him, it is a Technicolor show, complete with drama, thrills and frills. So, the inverted narcissist and the victims of narcissists (not all of them inverted narcissists), are attracted to excitement, to the violation of routine, to life itself. They live vicariously, by proxy, through their narcissist."

Relationships with Abusive Narcissists Online Chat Transcript
http://healthyplace.com/communities/personality_disorders/site/Transcripts/abusive_narcissists.htm

"Vaknin: The narcissist has alloplastic defences. What this means is that he tends to blame others, inanimate objects and people, for his behaviour. 'You made me do it' is a common sentence or, 'What could I do? I couldn't help it under the circumstances'. He is superstitious to some extent and paranoid ('The world/luck is against me').

Again, the key is simple: the narcissist is a vending machine. Input the coins of Narcissistic Supply and press the right button ('responsibility').

Example: the narcissist made a mistake. You want him to acknowledge his responsibility. Make the mistake GRAND, unprecedented, unique, amazing, stunning, and the narcissist will immediately 'adopt' it. Narcissistic Supply can be both negative or positive. To write the masterpiece of all time is the exact emotional equivalent of writing the flop of all time. To be a Hitler is identical to being Jesus. The narcissist has no moral or emotional preference between these two. He just wants to be considered the unique-est.

Sagui: Is there any report of a narcissist who, after a life crisis, cured completely?

Vaknin: Yes, a few in the literature. It was even suggested (1996) that there are two forms of narcissism: transient and permanent. I also think that we should distinguish between: reactive narcissism, narcissistic episode, NPD and narcissistic traits (or overlay).

David: Did the awareness of your Narcissistic Personality Disorder change anything about your 'real self'?

Vaknin: No, I have no access to my real self. I know as much as anyone about narcissism and it helped me none. To heal one must undergo an emotional transformation, to reach the point of the 'unbearable being', to want to change fervently. I have only my brain. This is one thing it is not good at: healing. In this sense, I am only a quarter human, an emotional quadriplegic. I had high hopes. I really wanted my brain to conquer my disorder. I studied. I wrote. I read. I fought with the only weapons I had and the only way I knew how. But it was the wrong war. I never got to meet the enemy.

lglritr: Dr. Vaknin, I'm in the process of a divorce from a narcissist who is the product of two extreme narcissist parents (one of which recently passed away). How do you protect an eleven year old child from their influence? I'm worried that I'm beginning to see an onset of some of the traits.

Vaknin: Nothing to do except serve as a counter-example. Show your kid that there is an alternative. That not all people are so self-centred and merciless in their pursuit of gratification. Be the kind of person you want him to be. Give him a choice. But do not choose for him because this is what narcissists do...:o)

Black Angel: My last relationship was with a narcissist. He was manipulating and controlling, often times without words, just a glance. Is this characteristic of NPDs? It is taking me a long time to regain my sense of self, and nature back. I feel that he drained me dry of everything good in me. Is this a natural feeling to have?

Vaknin: Yes and yes. Narcissists manipulate because they are control freaks and they are control freaks because they lost control early in life with devastating consequences. They manipulate verbally and behaviourally, and body language is an important weapon in their arsenal of communication. And, yes, your reaction is absolutely normal. You are sad (depressed?). You have gone through the trauma of being a Prisoner Of War. It was war, you know, not a relationship. You were fighting for your life and identity. For your sanity and his. For your relationship as you wanted it to be. So, now you have depression and PTSD. Get help. These two things are treatable, unlike narcissism."

Relationships with Abusive Narcissists Online Chat Transcript
http://healthyplace.com/communities/personality_disorders/site/Transcripts/abusive_narcissists.htm

"I want to tell you now what happens to narcissists when deprived of Narcissistic Supply of any kind (Secondary or Primary). Perhaps it will make it easier for you to understand why the narcissist pursues Narcissistic Supply so fervently, so relentlessly and so ruthlessly. Without Narcissistic Supply – the narcissist crumbles, he disintegrates like the zombies or the vampires in horror movies. It is terrifying and the narcissist will do anything to avoid it. Think about the narcissist as a drug addict. His withdrawal symptoms are identical: delusions, physiological effects, irritability, emotional lability."

The Magic of My Thinking - Sam Vaknin
http://samvak.tripod.com/journal6.html

"The narcissist derives his Narcissistic Supply from PNSS and SNSS (Primary and Secondary Narcissistic Supply Sources). But this supply is used by the narcissistic much the same as one uses perishable goods. He has to replenish this supply and, as is the case with other drug addictions, he has to increase the dosage as he goes. He uses the supply to substitute for certain ego functions (example: to regulate his self-esteem and sense of self-worth)."

The Concepts of Narcissistic Accumulation and Narcissistic Regulation - Sam Vaknin
http://samvak.tripod.com/msla7.html

"The narcissist feels good with his mate only when the narcissistic circumstances are good and the Narcissistic Supply is abundant. This is because his partner does not exist as a separate entity. She fulfils a function of mirroring (reflection). She continuously reflects to the narcissist the state of his Narcissistic Supply. The emotional content of the relationship alters in accordance with this state. Any effort on her part to change her role or to augment it; any time she ceases to behave as a function, or as an object - provoke conflict with the narcissist and aggression transformed and expressed through narcissistic rage."

The World of the Narcissist - Sam Vaknin
http://samvak.tripod.com/msla6.html

"Divorce is a life crisis - and more so for the narcissist. The narcissist stands to lose not only his spouse but an important Source of Narcissistic Supply. This results in narcissistic injury, rage, and an all-pervasive feelings of injustice, helplessness and paranoia."

Divorcing the Narcissist and the Psychopath - Sam Vaknin
http://samvak.tripod.com/5.html

"There are four categories of Narcissistic Supply Sources (NSS): ...
Mood disorders, compulsive rituals, substance abuse, paraphilias, reckless, or anti-social behaviour patterns often accompany pathological narcissism (they are co-morbid). While some of these coexistent problems can be ameliorated through a combination of medication and talk therapy - not so the core defence mechanisms of the narcissist."

Discussing Narcissism - Sam Vaknin
http://samvak.tripod.com/journal55.html

"Narcissists and Medication

Narcissists generally are averse to medication. It is an implied admission that something is wrong with them. Narcissists are control freaks and afraid to lose control. Additionally, many of them believe that medication is the 'great equalizer' – it will make them lose their uniqueness, superiority, and so on. That is UNLESS they can convincingly present taking the medication as an 'act of heroism', part of a daring enterprise of self exploration, a distinguishing feature of the narcissist and so on. They will often claim that the medicine affects them differently than it does other people, or that they have discovered a new, exciting way of using it, or that they are part of someone's (usually themselves) learning curve ('part of a new approach to dosage', 'part of a new cocktail which holds great promise'). Narcissists MUST dramatise their lives to feel worthy and special. Aut nihil aut unique – either be special or don't be at all.

Very much like in the physical world, change is brought about only through the incredible powers of torsion and breakage. Only when our elasticity gives way, only when we are wounded by our own intransigence – only then is there hope.

Most narcissists have simply not suffered enough. When they do – you find them courting therapists, studying their self, taking medicines, and changing. It takes nothing less than a real crisis. Ennui is not enough."

Excerpts from the Archives of the Narcissism List - Part 12 - Sam Vaknin
http://samvak.tripod.com/archive12.html

"NPD Son

An NPD son is no different to an NPD husband. You MUST devise and design survival strategies. Try to split his good sides from his less agreeable ones and avoid the latter to the best of your ability. Involve professional help. Being protective of him may be to his detriment.

Set your boundaries and stick to them. Be you, don't be fake, or play a part for his sake, or for the sake of domestic peace. Employ a balanced, just and predictable set of rewards and punishments. Educate him. If he becomes too onerous – get rid of him before he get rids of you. I am sorry to be so blunt but it is reality – not a textbook scenario."

Excerpts from the Archives of the Narcissism List - Part 12 - Sam Vaknin
http://samvak.tripod.com/archive12.html

"This kind of narcissist jealously guards his possessions – his collections, his furniture, his cars, his children, his women, his money, his credit cards... Objects comfort the narcissist."

The Objects of the Narcissist - Sam Vaknin
http://samvak.tripod.com/journal53.html

"Such a narcissist will say: 'My car is daring and unstoppable', or 'How clever is my computer!', or 'My dog is cunning', or 'My wife craves attention'. He often compares people to the inanimate. Himself he sees as a computer or sex machine. His wife he regards as some kind of luxury good. The narcissist loves objects and relates to them – things he fails to do with humans. This is why he objectifies people – it makes it easier for him to interact with them. Objects are predictable, reliable, always there, obedient, easy to control and manipulate, universally desired."

The Objects of the Narcissist - Sam Vaknin
http://samvak.tripod.com/journal53.html

"Objects, situations, voices, sights, colours – can provoke and evoke unwanted memories. The narcissist tries to avoid them. The discarder narcissist callously discards or gives away hard-won objects, memorabilia, gifts, and property. This behaviour sustains his sense of control and lack of vulnerability. It also proves to him that he is unique, not like 'other people' who are attached to their material belongings. He is above this."

The Objects of the Narcissist - Sam Vaknin
http://samvak.tripod.com/journal53.html

"Accumulator narcissists take to objects and memorabilia, to voices and tunes, to sights and to works of art – as reminders of their past glory and of their potential future grandeur. Many narcissists collect proofs and trophies of their sexual prowess, dramatic talent, past wealth, or intellectual achievements. They file them away almost compulsively. These are the Narcissistic Handles."

The Objects of the Narcissist - Sam Vaknin
http://samvak.tripod.com/journal53.html

"To counter this overwhelming feeling of helplessness (dependence on Narcissistic Supply), the narcissist becomes a control freak. He sadistically manipulates others to his needs. He derives pleasure from the utter subjugation of his human environment."

The Lonely Narcissist - Sam Vaknin
http://samvak.tripod.com/journal18.html

"Finally, the narcissist is a latent masochist. He seeks punishment, castigation and ex-communication. This self-destruction is the only way to validate powerful voices he internalised as a child ('You are a bad, rotten, hopeless child')."

The Lonely Narcissist - Sam Vaknin
http://samvak.tripod.com/journal18.html

"As you can easily see, the narcissistic landscape is fraught with contradictions. The narcissist depends on people - but hates and despises them. He wants to control them unconditionally - but is also looking to punish himself savagely. He is terrified of persecution ('persecutory delusions') - but seek the company of his own 'persecutors' compulsively. The narcissist is the victim of incompatible inner dynamics, ruled by numerous vicious circles, pushed and pulled simultaneously by irresistible forces."

The Lonely Narcissist - Sam Vaknin
http://samvak.tripod.com/journal18.html

"I lie. Compulsively and needlessly. All the time. About everything. And I often contradict myself. Why do I need to do this? To make myself interesting or attractive. In other words, to secure Narcissistic Supply (attention, admiration, adulation, gossip)."

Pseudologica Fantastica - Sam Vaknin
http://samvak.tripod.com/journal23.html

"I home in on the chinks in their laboriously constructed armours. I spot their Achilles' hill and attach to it. I prick the gas bags that most people are. I deflate them. I force them to confront their finiteness and helplessness and mediocrity. I negate their sense of uniqueness. I reduce them to proportion and provide them with a perspective. I do so cruelly and abrasively and sadistically and with lethal efficiency. I have no compassion. And I prey on their vulnerabilities, however microscopic, however well-concealed."

I Cannot Forgive - Sam Vaknin
http://samvak.tripod.com/journal24.html

"He induces unhappiness and gloom in others to enable him to experience his own misery."

The Happiness of Others - Sam Vaknin
http://samvak.tripod.com/others.html

"Last but not least, is the narcissist's exaggerated fear of losing control. The narcissist feels that he controls his human environment mostly by manipulation and mainly by emotional extortion and distortion."

The Happiness of Others - Sam Vaknin
http://samvak.tripod.com/others.html

"The somatic narcissist flaunts his sexual conquests, parades his possessions, exhibits his muscles, brags about his physical aesthetics or sexual prowess or exploits, is often a health freak and a hypochondriac. The cerebral narcissist is a know-it-all, haughty and intelligent 'computer'. He uses his awesome intellect, or knowledge (real or pretended) to secure adoration, adulation and admiration."

Dr. Jackal and Mr. Hide - Sam Vaknin
http://samvak.tripod.com/journal21.html

"The narcissist is incapable of loving, or even empathising with other people. To him, they are instruments in the compulsive pursuit of gratification, adulation, attention and affirmation (Narcissistic Supply). He does not fathom the human experience because his emotions are thoroughly repressed and he is obsessed with obtaining his 'drug' (the aforementioned supply)."

Narcissists, Violence and Abuse - Orientation Article - Sam Vaknin
http://www.suite101.com/article.cfm/npd/49236

"I make it a point to triumphantly ignore and belittle figures of authority. Knowing that their options of retaliation are rather limited by my official position, or by law - I abuse them flagrantly. When a security guard or a policeman halts me, I pretend I haven't heard him and proceed with callous disregard. When threatened, I go unpredictably wild. In doing so I (very often) provoke repulsion and pity and (much less often) fear and amazement. Often I find myself in danger, always punished, forever the losing party."

No One Counts to Ten - Sam Vaknin
http://samvak.tripod.com/journal28.html

"My inability to work in a team, to be instructed, to accept orders, to admit to ignorance, to listen to reason, and to succumb to social conventions, or to superior knowledge and credentials - transformed me into a reclusive and clownish disappointment. People are always misled by my intelligence into predicting a bright future for me and my work. I end up shattering their hopes. Mine is a heartless march to heartbreak."

No One Counts to Ten - Sam Vaknin
http://samvak.tripod.com/journal28.html

"I am constantly envious of people. This is my way of interacting with the world. I begrudge others their success, or brilliance, or happiness, or good fortune. I am driven to excesses of paranoia and guilt and fear that subside only after I 'act out' or punish myself. It is a vicious cycle in which I am entrapped."

The Green Eyed Narcissist - Sam Vaknin
http://samvak.tripod.com/journal19.html

"They feel worthy only of abasement and punishment. Besieged by guilt and remorse, voided of self-esteem, perpetually self-hating and self-deprecating - this is by far the more dangerous species of narcissist. For he who derives contentment from his own humiliation cannot but derive happiness from the downfall of others. Indeed, most of them end up driving the objects of their own devotion and adulation to destruction and decrepitude."

The Green Eyed Narcissist - Sam Vaknin
http://samvak.tripod.com/journal19.html

"And then, of course, there is my favourite solution: avoidance. To witness the success and joy of others is too painful, too high a price to pay. So, I stay home, alone and incommunicado. I inhabit the artificial bubble that is my world where I am king and country, I am the law and yardstick, I am the one and only. There, in the penumbral recesses of my study, my flickering laptop for company, the only noises are electronic and I am the resident of my own burgeoning delusions. I am happy and soothed. I am what I can dream and dream my very being. I am no longer real, simply a narrative, an invention of my fervent mind, a colourful myth - sustaining and engulfing. I am content."

The Green Eyed Narcissist - Sam Vaknin
http://samvak.tripod.com/journal19.html

"To the narcissist, other people are never more than potential Sources of Supply with a useful 'shelf life'. The narcissist invariably ends up cruelly devaluing and discarding them, like dysfunctional objects."

Discussions about Narcissism - Sam Vaknin
http://www.suite101.com/article.cfm/npd/93525

"Every aspect of the personality is pervaded by pathological narcissism. It colours the narcissist's behaviour, cognition, and emotional landscape. This ubiquity renders it virtually untreatable. Additionally, the narcissist develops deep-set resistance to authority figures, such as therapists. His attitude to treatment is conflictual, competitive, and hostile. When he fails to co-opt the therapist into upholding his grandiose self-image, the narcissist devalues and discards both the treatment and the mental health practitioner administering it."

Discussions about Narcissism - Sam Vaknin
http://www.suite101.com/article.cfm/npd/93525

"Pathological narcissism pervades every facet of the personality, every behaviour, every cognition, and every emotion. This makes it difficult to treat. Add to this the narcissist's unthinking and deeply-ingrained resistance to authority figures, such as therapists - and healing, or even mere behaviour modification, are rendered unattainable."

Discussions about Narcissism - Sam Vaknin
http://www.suite101.com/article.cfm/npd/93525

"Pathological narcissism is often co-morbid with mood disorders, compulsive rituals, substance abuse, paraphilias, or reckless behaviour patterns. Many narcissists are also anti-social. Lacking empathy and convinced of their own magnificence, they feel that they are above social conventions and the Law."

Discussions about Narcissism - Sam Vaknin
http://www.suite101.com/article.cfm/npd/93525

"The narcissist invents and nurtures a False Self intended to elicit attention - positive or negative - from others and thus to fill his innermost void. He is so engrossed in securing Narcissistic Supply from his sources by putting on an energy-sapping show - that he fails to materialise his potential, to have mature, adult relationships, to feel, and, in general, to enjoy life."

Discussing Narcissism - Sam Vaknin
http://samvak.tripod.com/journal55.html

"But more pernicious are the subtle and socially-acceptable forms of abuse - such as doting, smothering, treating the child as an extension of the parent, forcing the child to realise the parents' unfulfilled dreams and unrealised wishes, putting the child on constant display, maintaining unrealistic expectations of him and so on. These modes of abuse permeate the tenuous self-boundaries formed by the child and teach him that he is loved because of what he accomplishes rather than due to who he is."

Discussing Narcissism - Sam Vaknin
http://samvak.tripod.com/journal55.html

"To the narcissist, freedom, wealth, social status, family, vocation - are all means to an end. And the end is attention. If he can secure attention by being the big bad wolf - the narcissist will unhesitatingly transform himself into one."

Narcissism and Fraud - Sam Vaknin
http://www.suite101.com/article.cfm/npd/94269

"The balding, potbellied, narcissist still courts women aggressively. The impoverished tycoon sinks deeper into debts, trying to maintain an unsustainable and lavish lifestyle. The one-novel author or one-discovery scholar still demands professional deference and expects attention by media and superiors. The once-potent politician maintains regal airs and holds court in great pomp. The wizened actress demands special treatment and throws temper tantrums when rebuffed. The ageing beauty wears her daughter's clothes and regresses emotionally as she progresses chronologically."

Grandiosity Hangover and Narcissist Baiting - Sam Vaknin
http://www.suite101.com/article.cfm/npd/93772

"Cerebral narcissists sometimes go through somatic phases and somatic narcissists – if capable – adopt cerebral behaviour patterns. Their attitudes change accordingly. The temporarily somatic narcissist suddenly begins to exercise, groom himself, seduce, and have creative and imaginative sex. The somatic made cerebral tries to read more, becomes contemplative and a-social, and consumes culture. But these are passing phases and the narcissist always reverts to true – or should I say, false – form."

Physique Dysmorphique - Sam Vaknin
http://samvak.tripod.com/journal31.html

"The narcissist inflicts pain and suffering on his nearest and dearest: spouse, children, colleagues, employer, friends. While rarely physically violent, he is a master of mental torture and psychological nightmares."

Narcissists, Violence and Abuse - Orientation Article - Sam Vaknin
http://www.suite101.com/article.cfm/npd/49236

"People often mistake depression for emotion. They say: 'But you are sad' and they mean: 'But you are human', 'But you have emotions'. And this is wrong. True, depression is a big component in a narcissist's emotional makeup. But it mostly has to do with the absence of Narcissistic Supply. It mostly has to do with nostalgia to more plentiful days, full of adoration and attention and applause. It mostly occurs after the narcissist has depleted his Secondary Source of Narcissistic Supply (spouse, mate, girlfriend, colleagues) for a 'replay' of his days of glory. Some narcissists even cry – but they cry exclusively for themselves and for their lost paradise. And they do so conspicuously and publicly – to attract attention."

The Sad Dreams of the Narcissist - Sam Vaknin
http://samvak.tripod.com/journal17.html

"The narcissist is a human pendulum hanging by the thread of the void that is his False Self. He swings between brutal and vicious abrasiveness - and mellifluous, saccharine sentimentality. It is all a facsimile. Enough to fool the casual observer. Enough to extract the drug - other people's glances - the reflection that sustains this house of cards somehow."

The Sad Dreams of the Narcissist - Sam Vaknin
http://samvak.tripod.com/journal17.html

"I can intelligently discuss other emotions, which I never experienced - like empathy, or love - because I make it a point to read a lot and to correspond with people who claim to experience them."

The Music of My Emotions -Sam Vaknin
http://samvak.tripod.com/journal7.html

"I am a predator and you are the prey. Because I do not know what it is like to be you and I do not particularly care to know. Because my disorder is as essential to me as your feelings are to you. My normal state is my very illness. I look like you, I walk the walk and talk the talk and I - and my ilk - deceive you magnificently. Not out of the cold viciousness of our hearts - but because that is the way we are."

The Music of My Emotions -Sam Vaknin
http://samvak.tripod.com/journal7.html

"All the love in this world, and all the crusading women who think that they can 'fix' me by doling out their saccharine compassion and revolting 'understanding' and all the support and the holding environments and the textbooks - cannot change one iota in this maddening, self-imposed verdict meted out by the most insanely, obtusely, sadistically harsh judge: By me."

The Music of My Emotions -Sam Vaknin
http://samvak.tripod.com/journal7.html

"A narcissist rarely engages in self-directed, self-deprecating humour. If he does, he expects to be contradicted, rebuked and rebuffed by his listeners ('Come on, you are actually quite handsome!'), or to be commended or admired for his courage or for his wit and intellectual acerbity ('I envy your ability to laugh at yourself!'). As everything else in a narcissist's life, his sense of humour is deployed in the interminable pursuit of Narcissistic Supply."

The Self-Deprecating Narcissist - Sam Vaknin
http://www.suite101.com/article.cfm/npd/83666

"I can be self-deprecating and self-effacing. I do not recoil from making my dilapidated ego the target of my own barbs. Yet, this is true only when I have Narcissistic Supply aplenty. Narcissistic Supply – attention, adulation, admiration, applause, fame, celebrity, notoriety – neuter the sting of my self-directed jokes."

The Self-Deprecating Narcissist - Sam Vaknin
http://samvak.tripod.com/journal39.html

"I am completely different when I lack Narcissistic Supply or when in search of sources of such supply. Humour is always an integral part of my charm offensive. But, when Narcissistic Supply is deficient, it is never self-directed. Moreover, when deprived of supply, I react with hurt and rage when I am the butt of jokes and humorous utterances. I counter-attack ferociously and make a complete arse of myself."

The Self-Deprecating Narcissist - Sam Vaknin
http://www.suite101.com/article.cfm/npd/83666

"The Narcissistic Solution
    The substitution of the True Self with a False Self as in the Narcissistic Personality Disorder. The Schizotypal Personality Disorder largely belongs here too because of its fantastic and magical thinking. The Borderline Personality Disorder is a failed narcissistic solution. In BPD, the patient is aware (at least unconsciously) that the solution she adopted is 'not working'. This is the source of her anxiety and fear of abandonment. This gives rise to an identity disturbance, affective instability, suicidal ideation, and suicidal action, chronic feelings of emptiness, rage attacks, and transient (stress related) paranoid ideation."

Object Relations - The Psychology of Serial and Mass Killers
- Sam Vaknin
http://samvak.tripod.com/objectrelations.html

"A common error is to think that Narcissistic Supply consists only of admiration, adulation and positive feedback. Actually, being feared, or even derided is also Narcissistic Supply. The main element is attention."

> Object Relations - The Psychology of Serial and Mass Killers
> - Sam Vaknin
> http://samvak.tripod.com/objectrelations.html

"Terrorists, serial killers, and mass murderers can be phenomenologically described as narcissists in a constant state of deficient Narcissistic Supply."

> Object Relations - The Psychology of Serial and Mass Killers
> - Sam Vaknin
> http://samvak.tripod.com/objectrelations.html

"By all means: be angry, be upset (for good and just reasons) - and don't hesitate to communicate your displeasure. The narcissist needs guidance (he is disoriented) and this is one of the best ways of providing him with one."

> Responsibility and Other Matters - Sam Vaknin
> http://samvak.tripod.com/faq13.html

"This book strives to be my contribution to minimise the destruction caused by this disorder. (Listen to Dr. Vaknin as he describes the Narcissistic Personality Disorder and how it affects not only himself, but others.) - Audio link on this page."

> Malignant Self Love, Narcissism Revisited - Sam Vaknin
> http://www.narcissisticabuse.com/narcissismbook.html

"The narcissist lacks empathy - the ability to put himself in other people's shoes. He does not recognise boundaries - personal, corporate, or legal. Everything and everyone are to him mere instruments, extensions, objects unconditionally and uncomplainingly available in his pursuit of narcissistic gratification."

> Excerpts from the Archives of the Narcissism List - Part 39 - Sam Vaknin
> http://samvak.tripod.com/archive39.html

"One of the favourite tools of manipulation in the abuser's arsenal is the disproportional of his reactions. He reacts with supreme rage to the slightest slight. Or he would punish severely for what he perceives to be an offence against him, no matter how minor. Or, he would throw a temper tantrum over any discord or disagreement, however gently and considerately expressed. Or, he would act inordinately attentive, charming and tempting (even over-sexed, if need be).

This ever-shifting code of conduct and the unusually harsh and arbitrarily applied penalties are premeditated. The victims are kept in the dark. Neediness and dependence on the source of 'justice' meted and judgment passed – on the abuser – are thus guaranteed.

TIP

Demand a just and proportional treatment. Reject or ignore unjust and capricious behaviour. If you are up to the inevitable confrontation, react in kind. Let him taste some of his own medicine."

What is Abuse? - Sam Vaknin
http://samvak.tripod.com/abuse.html

"NPD is treated in talk therapy (psychodynamic or cognitive-behavioural). The prognosis for an adult narcissist is poor, though his adaptation to life and to others can improve with treatment. Medication is applied to side-effects and behaviours (such as mood or affect disorders and obsession-compulsion) – usually with some success."

Narcissistic Personality Disorder (NPD) at a Glance - Sam Vaknin
http://samvak.tripod.com/npdglance.html

"The narcissist's paranoid streak is likeliest to erupt when he lacks Narcissistic Supply. The regulation of his labile sense of self-worth is dependent upon external stimuli – adoration, adulation, affirmation, applause, notoriety, fame, infamy, and, in general, attention of any kind."

Grandiosity and Intimacy - The Roots of Paranoia - Sam Vaknin
http://www.suite101.com/article.cfm/npd/95897

"The paranoid narcissist ends life as an oddball recluse – derided, feared, and loathed in equal measures. His paranoia – exacerbated by repeated rejections and ageing – pervades his entire life and diminishes his creativity, adaptability, and functioning. The narcissist's personality, buffeted by paranoia, turns ossified and brittle. Finally, atomised and useless, it succumbs and gives way to a great void. The narcissist is consumed."

> Grandiosity and Intimacy - The Roots of Paranoia - Sam Vaknin
> http://www.suite101.com/article.cfm/npd/95897

"The paranoid delusions of the narcissist are always grandiose, 'cosmic', or 'historical'. His pursuers are influential and formidable. They are after his unique possessions, out to exploit his expertise and special traits, or to force him to abstain and refrain from certain actions. The narcissist feels that he is at the centre of intrigues and conspiracies of colossal magnitudes."

> Grandiosity and Intimacy - The Roots of Paranoia - Sam Vaknin
> http://www.suite101.com/article.cfm/npd/95897

"Narcissists are one-state machines, programmed to extract Narcissistic Supply from others. To do so, they develop early on a set of immutable routines. This propensity for repetition, this inability to change and rigidity confine the narcissist, stunt his development, and limit his horizons. Add to this his overpowering sense of entitlement, his visceral fear of failure, and his invariable need to both feel unique and be perceived as such – and one often ends up with a recipe for inaction."

> Whistling in the Dark - Sam Vaknin
> http://www.suite101.com/article.cfm/6514/95221

"The under-achieving narcissist dodges challenges, eludes tests, shirks competition, sidesteps expectations, ducks responsibilities, evades authority – because he is afraid to fail and because doing something everyone else does endangers his sense of uniqueness. Hence the narcissist's apparent 'laziness' and 'parasitism'. His sense of entitlement – with no commensurate accomplishments or investment – aggravates his milieu. People tend to regard such narcissists as 'spoiled brats'."

> Whistling in the Dark - Sam Vaknin
> http://www.suite101.com/article.cfm/6514/95221

"My advice to you is to immediately stop engaging in 'unconditional love'. Narcissists sense blood where others see only love and altruism. If – for masochistic reasons, which are beyond me – you still wish to engage this young person, my chief advice to you would be to condition your love. Sign a contract with him: you want my adoration, admiration, approval, warmth, you want my home and money available to you as an insurance policy? If you do – these are my conditions. And if he says that he doesn't want to have anything to do with you anymore – count your blessings and let go. Omar al-Khayyam, the famous Persian poet once wrote: when you want to have the bird – set it free."

Adolescent Narcissist - A Case Study - Sam Vaknin
http://samvak.tripod.com/faq16.html

"Question: If the narcissist is as abusive as you say – why do we react so badly when he leaves?

Answer: At the commencement of the relationship, the narcissist is a dream-come-true. He is often intelligent, witty, charming, good looking, an achiever, empathetic, in need of love, loving, caring, attentive and much more. Losing the narcissist is no different to any other major loss in life. It provokes a cycle of bereavement and grief (as well as some kind of mild Post-Traumatic Stress Syndrome in cases of severe abuse). This cycle has four phases: denial, rage, sadness and acceptance. At the healthier end of the spectrum of denial reactions is the classical denial of loss – the disbelief, the hope that the narcissist may return, the suspension and repression of all information to the contrary. This, in turn, gives place to gradual acceptance and renewed activity. The narcissist is gone both physically and mentally. The void left in his wake still hurts and pangs of regret and hope still exist. But, on the whole, the narcissist is transformed and the person entertains no delusions as to the one-sided and abusive nature of the relationship or as to the possibility and desirability of its renewal."

Mourning the Narcissist - Sam Vaknin
http://samvak.tripod.com/faq68.html

"It is difficult to let go of this idealised figure. Relationships with narcissists inevitably and invariably end with the dawn of a double realisation. The first is that one has been (ab)used by the narcissist and the second is that one was regarded by the narcissist as a disposable, dispensable and interchangeable instrument (object). The assimilation of this new gained knowledge is an excruciating process, often unsuccessfully completed. People get fixated at different stages. They fail to come to terms with their rejection as human beings – the most total form of rejection there is."

Mourning the Narcissist - Sam Vaknin
http://samvak.tripod.com/faq68.html

"The content of this Web site is based on correspondence since 1996 with hundreds of people suffering from the Narcissistic Personality Disorder (narcissists) and with thousands of their family members, friends, therapists, and colleagues."

How Can I Help You? - Sam Vaknin
http://malignantselflove.tripod.com/faq1.html

"My book says that narcissists are easily identifiable and that, once identified, can be easily manipulated. The need to manipulate them arises out of their propensity to destroy everything and everyone around them. To manipulate a narcissist is to survive. It is a survival tactic of the victims of narcissists."

My Story - Sam Vaknin
http://www.healthyplace.com/communities/personality_disorders/narcissism/about_me.html

"Question: Does narcissism often occur with other mental health disorders (co-morbidity) or with substance abuse (dual diagnosis)?
Answer: NPD (Narcissistic Personality Disorder) is often diagnosed with other mental health disorders (such as the Borderline, Histrionic, or Antisocial Personality Disorder). This is called 'co-morbidity'. It is also often accompanied by substance abuse and other reckless and impulsive behaviours and this is called 'dual diagnosis'."

Narcissism with Other Mental Health Disorders
(Co-Morbidity and Dual Diagnosis) - Sam Vaknin
http://samvak.tripod.com/faq82.html

"Aware of impending loss and doom, the narcissist embarks on a charm offensive, parading the most irresistible, brilliant, captivating, titillating, promising and thrilling aspects of his False

Self. The aim is to reacquire that which has been forfeited to neglect and indifference, to rebuild relationships ruined by contempt and abuse – and, thus, to regain the mislaid fount of Narcissistic Supply."

Losing for Granted - Sam Vaknin
http://www.suite101.com/article.cfm/npd/97355

"Question: What is the effect that a narcissist parent has on his offspring?

Answer: At the risk of over-simplification: narcissism tends to breed narcissism. Only a minority of the children of narcissistic parents become narcissists. This may be due to genetic predisposition or different life circumstances (like not being firstborn). But MOST narcissists had one or more narcissistic parents or caregivers."

Narcissistic Parents - Sam Vaknin
http://samvak.tripod.com/faq5.html

"Perhaps I am the one who came along and built you up when you were down, employed you when you were out of a job, showed the way when you were lost, offered confidence when you were doubting, made you laugh when you were blue, sparked your interest when you were bored, listened to you and understood, saw you for what you really are, felt your pain and found the answers, made you want to be alive. Of course you recognise me. I am your inspiration, your role model, your saviour, your leader, your best friend, the one you aspire to emulate, the one whose favour makes you glow. But I can also be your worst nightmare."

Introduction to "Malignant Self Love - Narcissism Revisited"
- Ken Heilbrunn, M.D.
http://samvak.tripod.com/kenintro.html

"Run to our friends. Go. See what that will get you. Ridicule. I am to them what I originally was to you. They believe what they see."

Introduction to "Malignant Self Love - Narcissism Revisited"
- Ken Heilbrunn, M.D.
http://samvak.tripod.com/kenintro.html

"Hello. Recognise me? No? Well, you see me all the time. You read my books, watch me on the big screen, feast on my art, cheer at my games, use my inventions, vote me into office, follow me into battle... Of course you recognise me. I am your inspiration, your role model, your saviour, your leader, your best friend, the one you aspire to emulate, the one whose favour makes you glow. But I can also be your worst nightmare."

                    Introduction to "Malignant Self Love - Narcissism Revisited"
                                            - Ken Heilbrunn, M.D.
                              http://samvak.tripod.com/kenintro.html

"I am your inspiration, your role model, your saviour, your leader, your best friend, the one you aspire to emulate, the one whose favour makes you glow. But I can also be your worst nightmare. If by chance you get caught in my web, I can make your life a living hell. But remember this. I am in that web too. The difference between you and me is that you can get out."

                    Introduction to "Malignant Self Love - Narcissism Revisited"
                                              - Ken Heilbrunn, M.D.
                              http://samvak.tripod.com/kenintro.html

"You really are incompetent, disrespectful, untrustworthy, immoral, ignorant, inept, egotistical, constrained, disgusting. You are a social embarrassment, an unappreciative partner, an inadequate parent, a disappointment, a sexual flop, a financial liability. I tell you this to your face. I must. It is my right, because it is. I behave, at home and away, any way I want to, with total disregard for conventions, mores, or the feelings of others."

                    Introduction to "Malignant Self Love - Narcissism Revisited"
                                            - Ken Heilbrunn, M.D.
                              http://samvak.tripod.com/kenintro.html

"First I build you up because that's what you need. Your skies are blue. Then, out of the blue, I start tearing you down. You let me do it because that's what you are used to."

                    Introduction to "Malignant Self Love - Narcissism Revisited"
                                          - Ken Heilbrunn, M.D.
                              http://samvak.tripod.com/kenintro.html

"Those eruptions of anger you dread and fear, my rages. Ah, it feels so good to rage. It is the expression of and the confirmation of my power over you."

Introduction to "Malignant Self Love - Narcissism Revisited"
- Ken Heilbrunn, M.D.
http://samvak.tripod.com/kenintro.html

"Lying feels good too, for the same reason, but nothing compares to the pleasure of exploding for no material reason and venting my anger like a lunatic, all the time a spectator at my own show and seeing your helplessness, pain, fear, frustration, and dependence. Go ahead. Tell our friends about it. See if they can imagine it, let alone believe it. The more outrageous your account of what happened, the more convinced they will be that the crazy one is you."

Introduction to "Malignant Self Love - Narcissism Revisited"
- Ken Heilbrunn, M.D.
http://samvak.tripod.com/kenintro.html

"The more outrageous your account of what happened, the more convinced they will be that the crazy one is you. And don't expect much more from your therapist either. Surely it is easier to live my lie and see where that takes you. You might even acquire some of the behaviour you find so objectionable in me."

Introduction to "Malignant Self Love - Narcissism Revisited"
- Ken Heilbrunn, M.D.
http://samvak.tripod.com/kenintro.html

"I am, as I said, my own worst nightmare. True, the world is replete with my contributions, and I am lots of fun to be around. And true, most contributions like mine are not the result of troubled souls. But many more than you might want to believe are. And if by chance you get caught in my web, I can make your life a living hell. But remember this. I am in that web too. The difference between you and me is that you can get out."

Introduction to "Malignant Self Love - Narcissism Revisited"
- Ken Heilbrunn, M.D.
http://samvak.tripod.com/kenintro.html

"How many others like me are there? More than you might think, and our numbers are increasing. Take twenty people off the street and you will find one whose mind ticks so much like mine that you could consider us clones. Impossible, you say. But it is. That is the enlightenment of Narcissism Revisited by Sam Vaknin. Sam is himself one such clone. What distinguishes him is his uncharacteristic courage to confront, and his uncanny understanding of, that which makes us tick, himself included. Not only does Sam dare ask and then answer the question we clones avoid like the plague, he does so with relentless, laser-like precision.

Read his book. Take your seat at the double-headed microscope and let Sam guide you through the dissection. Like a brain surgeon operating on himself, Sam explores and exposes the alien among us, hoping beyond hope for a resectable tumour but finding instead each and every cell teaming with the same resistant virus. The operation is long and tedious, and at times frightening and hard to believe. Read on. The parts exposed are as they are, despite what may seem hyperbolic or far fetched. Their validity might not hit home until later, when coupled with memories of past events and experiences."

Introduction to "Malignant Self Love - Narcissism Revisited"
- Ken Heilbrunn, M.D.
http://samvak.tripod.com/kenintro.html

"How many others like me are there? More than you might think, and our numbers are increasing. Take twenty people off the street and you will find one whose mind ticks so much like mine that you could consider us clones. Impossible, you say. It is simply not possible for that many people – highly accomplished, respected, and visible people – to be out there replacing reality with illusions, each in the same way and for reasons they know not why. It is simply not possible for so many robots of havoc and chaos, as I describe them, to function daily midst other educated, intelligent, and experienced individuals, and pass for normal."

Introduction to "Malignant Self Love - Narcissism Revisited"
- Ken Heilbrunn, M.D.
http://samvak.tripod.com/kenintro.html

"It is simply not possible for such an aberration of human cognition and behaviour to infiltrate and infect the population in such numbers, virtually undetected by the radar of mental health professionals. It is simply not possible for so much visible positive to contain so much concealed negative. It is simply not possible. But it is."

Introduction to "Malignant Self Love - Narcissism Revisited"
- Ken Heilbrunn, M.D.
http://samvak.tripod.com/kenintro.html

"And I am constantly taking fan club inventory, testing the loyalty of present members with challenges of abuse, writing off defectors with total indifference, and scouting the landscape for new recruits. Do you see my dilemma? I use people who are dependent on me to keep my illusions alive. In actuality it is I who am dependent on them. Even the rage, that orgasmic release of pain and anger, doesn't work without an audience."

Introduction to "Malignant Self Love - Narcissism Revisited"
- Ken Heilbrunn, M.D.
http://samvak.tripod.com/kenintro.html

"The NPD is a newcomer to the zoo of mental disorders. It was not fully defined until the late 1980's. The discussion, analysis and study of narcissism are as old as psychology - but there is a great difference between being a 'mere' narcissist and having a NPD. So, no one has a clue as to how widespread this particular personality disorder is - or, even, how widespread personality disorders are (estimates range between 3 and 15% of the population. I think 5-7% would be a fair ballpark figure)."

An Overview of the Narcissist - Sam Vaknin
http://samvak.tripod.com/faq2.html

"Thus, if recurrently traumatised or abused by external or internal forces, a group of people may develop the mass equivalent of pathological narcissism as a defence or compensatory mechanism."

Narcissists, Group Behaviour, and Terrorism
- Interview with Sam Vaknin
http://samvak.tripod.com/12.html

"The 'small people', the 'rank and file', the 'loyal soldiers' of the narcissist - his flock, his nation, his employees - they pay the price. The disillusionment and disenchantment are agonising. The process of reconstruction, of rising from the ashes, of overcoming the trauma of having been deceived, exploited and manipulated - is drawn-out. It is difficult to trust again, to have faith, to love, to be led, to collaborate. Feelings of shame and guilt engulf the erstwhile followers of the narcissist. This is his sole legacy: a massive Post-Traumatic Stress Disorder."

Narcissistic Leaders - Sam Vaknin
http://samvak.tripod.com/15.html

"Cooked books, corporate fraud, bending the (accounting or other) rules, sweeping problems under the carpet, over-promising, making grandiose claims - are hallmarks of a narcissist in action."

Narcissism in the Boardroom - Part II - Sam Vaknin
http://www.upi.com/view.cfm?StoryID=20021021-101212-2299r

"He constantly lies about every aspect of his life: his self, his history, his vocation and avocations, his emotions. This false information and the informative asymmetry in the relationship guarantee his informative lead, or 'advantage'."

Uniqueness and Intimacy - Sam Vaknin
http://samvak.tripod.com/msla2.html

"Many narcissists reject treatment even in the most dire circumstances. Feeling omnipotent, they seek the answers themselves and in themselves and then venture to 'fix' and 'maintain' themselves. They read, gather information, philosophise and contemplate. They do all this single-handedly and when they seek other people's counsel, they degrade them and treat them as sheer 'human information sources'."

The World of the Narcissist - Sam Vaknin
http://samvak.tripod.com/msla1.html

"Only people whose Ego is underdeveloped and relatively undifferentiated need ever larger quantities of external ego boundary setting, of affirmation through reflection. To them, there is no distinction between meaningful and less meaningful others. Everyone carries the same weight and fulfils the same functions: reflection, affirmation, recognition, adulation, or attention. This is why everyone is interchangeable and dispensable."

The World of the Narcissist - Sam Vaknin
http://samvak.tripod.com/msla1.html

"The blissfully ignorant are simply unaware of the 'bad sides' of the narcissist- and make sure they remain so. They look the other way, or pretend that the narcissist's behaviour is normative, or turn a blind eye to his egregious misbehaviour. They are classic deniers of reality. Some of them maintain a generally rosy outlook premised on the inbred benevolence of Mankind. Others simply cannot tolerate dissonance and discord. They prefer to live in a fantastic world where everything is harmonious and smooth and evil is banished. They react with rage to any information to the contrary and block it out instantly. This type of denial is well evidenced in dysfunctional families."

Facilitating Narcissism - Sam Vaknin
http://www.suite101.com/article.cfm/npd/97535

"The deceived are people - or institutions, or collectives - deliberately taken for a premeditated ride by the narcissist. He feeds them false information, manipulates their judgement, proffers plausible scenarios to account for his indiscretions, soils the opposition, charms them, appeals to their reason, or to their emotions, and promises the moon. Again, the narcissist's incontrovertible powers of persuasion and his impressive personality play a part in this predatory ritual. The deceived are especially hard to deprogram. They are often themselves encumbered with narcissistic traits and find it impossible to admit a mistake, or to atone. They are likely to stay on with the narcissist to his - and their - bitter end. Regrettably, the narcissist rarely pays the price for his offences. His victims pick up the tab. But even here the malignant optimism of the abused never ceases to amaze."

Facilitating Narcissism - Sam Vaknin
http://www.suite101.com/article.cfm/npd/97535

"Even the official termination of a relationship with a narcissist is not the end of the affair. The Ex 'belongs' to the narcissist. She is an inseparable part of his Pathological Narcissistic Space. This possessive streak is not terminated with the official, physical, separation. Thus, the narcissist is likely to respond with rage, seething envy, a sense of humiliation and invasion and violent-aggressive urges to an ex's new boyfriend, or new job (to her new life without him). Especially since it implies a 'failure' on his part and, thus negates his grandiosity."

The Neverending Story - Sam Vaknin
http://samvak.tripod.com/faq80.html

"The personality disordered devote any shred of vitality to the projection and maintenance of a False Self, whose sole purpose is to elicit attention, admiration, approval, acknowledgement, fear, or adulation from others."

The Energy of Self - Sam Vaknin
http://samvak.tripod.com/journal57.html

"To the abuser, losing control means going insane. Because other people are mere elements in the abuser's mind - being unable to manipulate them literally means losing it (his mind). Imagine, if you suddenly were to find out that you cannot manipulate your memories or control your thoughts... Nightmarish! In his frantic efforts to maintain control or re-assert it, the abuser resorts to a myriad of fiendishly inventive stratagems and mechanisms."

What is Abuse? - Sam Vaknin
http://samvak.tripod.com/abuse.html

"'Pure' NPDs do not enjoy hurting others - but they do enjoy the sensation of omnipotence, unlimited power and the validation of their grandiose fantasies when they hurt others or in the position to do so. It is more the POTENTIAL to hurt others than the actual act that turns them on."

The Narcissist - Sam Vaknin
http://www.atthefence.com/AUGUST2001/8Narcissist.htm

"The malignant narcissist invents and then projects a false, fictitious, self for the world to fear, or to admire."

Narcissistic Leaders - Sam Vaknin
http://samvak.tripod.com/15.html

"The only way not to be harmed by a narcissist is not to interact with one. AT ALL. Narcissist sense your weaknesses and attack them viciously and rapaciously. They are dangerous predators. One does not compromise with a tiger or accommodates a snake."

Excerpts from the Archives of the Narcissism List - Part 26 - Sam Vaknin
http://samvak.tripod.com/archive26.html

"I am not a physical type, so I will never harm a woman physically. But, wherever possible to inflict pain and to drive a woman to the limits of her sanity - I do a good job of it."

Excerpts from the Archives of the Narcissism List - Part 26 - Sam Vaknin
http://samvak.tripod.com/archive26.html

"Narcissists are sadists and inverted narcissists are both rare and the perfect match."

Excerpts from the Archives of the Narcissism List - Part 26 - Sam Vaknin
http://samvak.tripod.com/archive26.html

"Narcissists abhor and dread getting emotionally intimate. The cerebral ones regard sex as a maintenance chore, something they have to do in order to keep their Source of Secondary Supply. The somatic narcissist treats women as objects and sex as a means to obtaining Narcissistic Supply."

Narcissists and Women - Sam Vaknin
http://samvak.tripod.com/faq79.html

"Moreover, many narcissists tend to engage in FRUSTRATING behaviours towards women. They refrain from having sex with them, tease them and then leave them, resist flirtatious and seductive behaviours and so on. Often, they invoke the existence of a girlfriend/fiancée/spouse (or boyfriend/etc. - male and female are interchangeable in my texts) as the 'reason' why they cannot have sex/develop a relationship. But this is not out of loyalty and fidelity in the empathic and loving sense. This is because they wish (and often succeed) to sadistically frustrate the interested party."

Narcissists and Women - Sam Vaknin
http://samvak.tripod.com/faq79.html

"Torture is the ultimate act of perverted intimacy. The torturer invades the victim's body, pervades his psyche, and possesses his mind. Deprived of contact with others and starved for human interactions, the prey bonds with the predator. 'Traumatic bonding', akin to the Stockholm Syndrome, is about hope and the search for meaning in the brutal and indifferent and nightmarish Universe of the torture cell."

The Psychology of Torture - Sam Vaknin
http://samvak.tripod.com/torturepsychology.html

"The narcissist is shallow, a pond pretending to be an ocean. He likes to think of himself as a Renaissance man, a Jack of all trades. A narcissist never admits to ignorance IN ANY FIELD!"

How to Recognise a Narcissist? - Sam Vaknin
http://samvak.tripod.com/faq58.html

"The best – really, the only way – a narcissist can help himself is by applying to a mental health professional. Even then, sadly, the prognosis and the healing prospects are dim. It seems that only time can bring on a limited remission (or, at times, aggravation of the condition). Therapy can tackle the more pernicious aspects of this disorder. It can help the patient to adapt to his condition, to accept it and to learn to conduct a more functional life with it. Learning to live with one's disorder – is a great achievement and the narcissist should be happy that even this modicum of success is, in principle, possible."

Can a Narcissist Help Himself? - Sam Vaknin
http://samvak.tripod.com/faq31.html

"The False Self is misrepresented by the narcissist as his True Self. The narcissist is saying, in effect: 'I am not who you think that I am. I am someone else. I am that (False) Self. Therefore, I deserve a better, painless, more considerate treatment'. The False Self, thus, is a contraption intended to alter the attitude of the (human) environment towards the narcissist."

The Dual Role of the False Self - Sam Vaknin
http://samvak.tripod.com/faq48.html

"The narcissist is possessed of an uncanny ability to psychologically penetrate others. Often, this gift is abused and put at the service of the narcissist's control freakery and sadism. The narcissist uses it liberally to annihilate the natural defences of his victims by faking unprecedented, almost inhuman, empathy. This capacity is coupled with the narcissist's ability to frighteningly imitate emotions and their attendant behaviours. The narcissist possesses 'emotional resonance tables'. He keeps records of every action and reaction, every utterance and consequence, every datum provided by others regarding their state of mind and emotional makeup. From these, he then constructs a set of formulas, which often result in impeccably and eerily accurate renditions of emotional behaviour. This can be enormously deceiving."

The Dual Role of the False Self - Sam Vaknin
http://samvak.tripod.com/faq48.html

"People have a need to believe in the empathic skills and basic good-heartedness of others. By dehumanising and objectifying people – the abuser attacks the very foundations human interaction. This is the 'alien' aspect of abusers – they may be excellent imitations of fully formed adults but they are emotionally absent and immature. Abuse is so horrid, so repulsive, so phantasmagoric – that people recoil in terror. It is then, with their defences absolutely down, that they are the most susceptible and vulnerable to the abuser's control. Physical, psychological, verbal and sexual abuse are all forms of dehumanisation and objectification."

What is Abuse? - Sam Vaknin
http://samvak.tripod.com/abuse.html

"The reason narcissism was under-reported and healing over-stated was that therapists have been fooled by smart narcissists. Most narcissists are expert manipulators and they learned how to deceive the therapists. You can see this very often in prison."

Treatment Modalities and Therapies - Sam Vaknin
http://samvak.tripod.com/faq77.html

"The source of all the narcissist's problems is the foreboding sensation that human relationships invariably end in humiliation, betrayal, pain and abandonment. This belief is embedded in them during their very early childhood by their parents, peers, or role models."

The World of the Narcissist - Sam Vaknin
http://samvak.tripod.com/msla8.html

"Question: How do narcissists react to being humiliated?
   Answer: As healthy human beings do – only more so, much more so."

Narcissistic Humiliation - Sam Vaknin
http://samvak.tripod.com/faq53.html

"Question: Can you provide us with some statistics? How often does bullying occur? How many people are affected?
   Answer: Surveys of bullying in the United Kingdom indicate that between 12-50 percent of the workforce experience bullying. Statistics from the U.K. National Workplace Bullying Advice Line reveal that around 20 percent of cases are from the education sector, 12 percent are from healthcare, 10 percent are from social services and around 6 percent from the voluntary, charity, not-for-profit sector. After that, calls come from all sectors both public and private, with finance, media, police, postal workers and other government employees featuring prominently. Enquiries from outside the United Kingdom – notably the United States, Canada, Australia and Ireland – show similar patterns with the caring professions topping the list of bullied workers."

Bully at Work - Interview with Tim Field by Dr. Sam Vaknin
http://www.upi.com/view.cfm?StoryID=25022002-100833-5315r

"When unable to secure 'normal' Narcissistic Supply – adulation, recognition, fame, celebrity, notoriety, infamy, affirmation, or mere attention – the narcissist resorts to 'abnormal' Narcissistic Supply. He tries to obtain his drug – the thrills, the good feeling that comes with Narcissistic Supply – by behaving recklessly, by succumbing to substance abuse, or by living dangerously."

The Adrenaline Junkie - Sam Vaknin
http://www.suite101.com/article.cfm/npd/99584

"When confronted with a boring, routine existence – with a chronic and permanent inability to secure Narcissistic Supply and excitement - these people compensate by inventing thrills where there are none."

The Adrenaline Junkie - Sam Vaknin
http://www.suite101.com/article.cfm/npd/99584

"Question: How does the narcissist treat his past Sources of Narcissistic Supply?
Answer: One should be careful not to romanticise the narcissist. His remorse is always linked to fears of losing his sources. Narcissists have no enemies. They have only Sources of Narcissistic Supply. An enemy means attention means supply. One holds sway over one's enemy. If the narcissist has the power to provoke emotions in you - you are still a Source of Supply to him, regardless of WHICH emotions are provoked."

Narcissists, Narcissistic Supply and Sources of Supply - Sam Vaknin
http://samvak.tripod.com/faq76.html

"The narcissist regards himself as one would an expensive present: a gift to his company, family, neighbours, colleagues or country. This firm conviction of his inflated importance makes him feel entitled to special treatment, special outcomes, immediate gratification, obsequiousness, and leniency. It also makes him feel immune to mortal laws and somehow divinely protected and insulated from the inevitable consequences of his deeds and misdeeds."

Analysis - Narcissism in the Boardroom - Sam Vaknin
http://www.upi.com/view.cfm?StoryID=20021018-013859-4113r

"Some narcissists are raised by weak or inaccessible mothers and harsh, rigid, or sadistic fathers. They tend to bond with males in male settings (army, sports, police, bodybuilding, the Catholic Church)."

Do Narcissists Hate Women? - Sam Vaknin
http://samvak.tripod.com/6.html

"Moreover, it is important to distinguish between the traits and behaviour patterns that are independent of the patient's cultural-social context (i.e., inherent, or idiosyncratic) - and reactive patterns, or conformity to cultural and social mores and edicts.

Reactions to severe life crises are often characterised by transient pathological narcissism, for instance (Ronningstam and Gunderson, 1996). But such reactions do not a narcissist make."

Telling Them Apart - Sam Vaknin
http://samvak.tripod.com/journal63.html

"Narcissists are either compulsively driven over-achievers – or chronic under-achieving wastrels. Most of them fail to make full and productive use of their potential and capacities. Many avoid even the now standard path of an academic degree, a career, or family life. The disparity between the accomplishments of the narcissist and his grandiose fantasies and inflated self image – the Grandiosity Gap – is staggering and, in the long run, insupportable. It imposes onerous exigencies on the narcissist's grasp of reality and social skills. It pushes him either to seclusion or to a frenzy of 'acquisitions' – cars, women, wealth, power."

Whistling in the Dark - Sam Vaknin
http://samvak.tripod.com/journal58.html

"Pathological narcissism is the art of deception. The narcissist projects a False Self and manages all his social interactions through this concocted fictional construct. People often find themselves involved with a narcissist (emotionally, in business, or otherwise) before they have a chance to discover his true nature."

Telling Them Apart - Sam Vaknin
http://samvak.tripod.com/journal63.html

"The narcissist objectifies people and treats them as expendable commodities to be discarded after use. Admittedly, that, in itself, is evil. Yet, it is the mechanical, thoughtless, heartless face of narcissistic abuse – devoid of human passions and of familiar emotions – that renders it so alien, so frightful and so repellent."

Narcissism and Evil - Sam Vaknin
http://www.suite101.com/article.cfm/npd/100724

"We are often shocked less by the actions of narcissist than by the way he acts. In the absence of a vocabulary rich enough to capture the subtle hues and gradations of the spectrum of narcissistic depravity, we default to habitual adjectives such as 'good' and 'evil'. Such intellectual laziness does this pernicious phenomenon and its victims little justice.

The narcissist is able to tell right from wrong and to distinguish between good and evil. In the pursuit of his interests and causes, he sometimes chooses to act wickedly. Lacking empathy, the narcissist is rarely remorseful. Because he feels entitled, exploiting others is second nature. The narcissist abuses others absent-mindedly, offhandedly, as a matter of fact."

Narcissism and Evil - Sam Vaknin
http://www.suite101.com/article.cfm/npd/100724

"Money, compliments, a favourable critique, an appearance in the media, a sexual intercourse are all transformed into the same currency in the narcissist's mind. This currency is what I call Narcissistic Supply."

The Concept of Narcissistic Supply - Sam Vaknin
http://samvak.tripod.com/msla6.html

"Know and accept thyself. This is what you are. You are highly intelligent. You are very inquisitive. You are a narcissist. These are facts. Narcissism is an adaptive mechanism. It is dysfunctional – but it saves you from a LOT MORE dysfunction or even a-function. Make a list: What does it mean to be a narcissist in your specific case? What are your typical behaviour patterns? Which types of behaviour are counterproductive, irritating, self-defeating or self-destructive? Which are productive, constructive and should be enhanced DESPITE their pathological origin?"

Taming the Beast: Pathological Narcissism and the Quality of Life
- Sam Vaknin
http://www.mental-health-matters.com/articles/article.php?artID=204

"Because of his lack of empathy and his rigid personality he often inflicts great (physical or mental) pain on meaningful others in his life – and he enjoys their writhing and suffering. In this restricted sense he is a sadist."

The Narcissist as Sadist - Sam Vaknin
http://samvak.tripod.com/faq56.html

"Other disorders, like Bi-polar (mania-depression), are characterised by mood swings NOT brought about by external events (endogenic, not exogenic). The narcissist's mood swings are only the results of external events (as he perceives and interprets them, of course)."

> Excerpts from the Archives of the Narcissism List - Part 3 - Sam Vaknin
> http://samvak.tripod.com/archive03.html

"The Narcissist avoids 'emotional handles': photographs, music identified with a certain period in his life, places, people, mementoes and emotional situations. The narcissist lives on borrowed time in a borrowed life. Every place and time period are but transitory (sufficient but not necessary) and lead to the next, unfamiliar environment. The narcissist feels that the end is near. He lives in rented apartments, is an illegal immigrant in many countries, works without the necessary permits and licenses, is fully mobile on a short notice, does not buy real estate or immovables. He travels light and he likes to travel."

> The Entitlement of Routine - Sam Vaknin
> http://samvak.tripod.com/journal10.html

"Pathological narcissism is an addiction to Narcissistic Supply, the narcissist's drug of choice. It is, therefore, not surprising that other addictive and reckless behaviours - workaholism, alcoholism, drug abuse, pathological gambling, compulsory shopping, or reckless driving - piggyback on this primary dependence."

> Narcissism, Substance Abuse, and Reckless Behaviours - Sam Vaknin
> http://www.suite101.com/article.cfm/npd/101146

"The somatic finds cyber-sex and cyber-relationships aplenty. The cerebral claims false accomplishments, fake skills, erudition and talents."

> The Cyber Narcissist - Sam Vaknin
> http://www.suite101.com/article.cfm/npd/101392

"It is at this stage that the risk of child abuse - up to and including outright incest - is heightened. The narcissist is auto-erotic. He is the preferred object of his own sexual attraction. His siblings and his children share his genetic material. Molesting or having intercourse with them is as close as the narcissist gets to having sex with himself."

> The Narcissist and His Family - Sam Vaknin
> http://samvak.tripod.com/faq22.html

"Having sex with a first-degree blood relative is like having sex with yourself. It is a narcissistic act and like all acts narcissistic, it involves the objectification of the partner. The incestuous narcissist over-values and then devalues his sexual partner. He is devoid of empathy (cannot see the other's point of view or put himself in her shoes)."

> On the Incest Taboo - Sam Vaknin
> http://www.healthyplace.com/communities/personality_disorders/narcissism/incest.html

"Money stands for love in the narcissist's emotional vocabulary. Having been deprived of love early on in his childhood, the narcissist constantly seeks for love substitutes. To him, money is THE love substitute. All the qualities of the narcissist are manifest in his relationship with money, and in his attitude towards it. Due to his sense of entitlement – he feels that he is entitled to other people's money. His grandiosity leads him to believe that he should have, or does have more money than he actually has. This leads to reckless spending, to pathological gambling, to substance abuse, or to compulsive shopping. Their magical thinking leads narcissists to irresponsible and short-sighted behaviour, the results of which they believe themselves to be immune from. So, they descend to debt, they commit financial crimes, they hassle people, including their closest relatives. Their fantasies lead them to believe in financial (fabricated) 'facts' (achievements) – incommensurate with their talents, qualifications, jobs, and resources. They pretend to be richer than they are, or capable of becoming rich, if they so resolve. They have a love-hate ambivalent relationship with money. They are mean, stingy, and calculating with their own money – and spendthrift with OPM (other people's money). They live lavishly, well above their means. The often go bankrupt and ruin their businesses. Reality very rarely matches their grandiose fantasies. Nowhere is the Grandiosity Gap more evident than where money is involved."

> Excerpts from the Archives of the Narcissism List - Part 15 - Sam Vaknin
> http://samvak.tripod.com/archive15.html

"What to Tell Your Narcissist?
I would tell him that we are all shaped in our early childhood by people: parents, teachers, other adults, our peers. It is a delicate job of fine tuning. Very often it is incomplete or wrongly done. As children, we defend ourselves against the incompetence (and, sometimes, the abuse) of our elders. We are individuals, so we each adopt (often unconsciously) a different defence mechanism. One of these self-defence mechanisms is called 'narcissism'. It is the choice not to seek love and acceptance from – and not to give them to – those incapable or unwilling to provide it. Instead, we construct an imaginary 'self'. It is everything that we are not, as children. It is omnipotent, omniscient, immune, grandiose, fantastic and ideal. We direct our love at this creation. But deep inside, we know that it is our invention. We need others to inform us constantly and persuasively that it is not MERELY our invention, that it has an existence all of its own, independent of us. This is why we look for Narcissistic Supply: attention, adoration, admiration, applause, approval, affirmation, fame, power, sex, etc."

Excerpts from the Archives of the Narcissism List – Part 15 – Sam Vaknin
http://samvak.tripod.com/archive15.html

"Treat the narcissists as you would children. This is so CLEAR and so endearing. It fosters in many the wish to protect the narcissist from his own delusions or to violently shake him into submission for his own good."

Excerpts from the Archives of the Narcissism List – Part 15 – Sam Vaknin
http://samvak.tripod.com/archive15.html

"The abuser may be functional or dysfunctional, a pillar of society, or a peripatetic con-artist, rich or poor, young or old. There is no universally-applicable profile of the 'typical abuser'. Yet, abusive behaviour often indicates serious underlying psychopathologies."

Danse Macabre – The Dynamics of Spousal Abuse – Sam Vaknin
http://www.suite101.com/article.cfm/18046/101460

"The abuser – stealthily but unfailingly – exploits the vulnerabilities in the psychological makeup of his victim. The abused party may have low self-esteem, a fluctuating sense of self-worth, primitive defence mechanisms, phobias, mental health problems, a disability, a history of failure, or a tendency to blame herself (autoplastic neurosis). She may have come from an abusive family or environment – which conditioned her to expect abuse as inevitable and 'normal'. In extreme and rare cases – the victim is a masochist, possessed of an urge to seek ill-treatment and pain."

Danse Macabre - The Dynamics of Spousal Abuse - Sam Vaknin
http://www.suite101.com/article.cfm/18046/101460

"Question: Should I tell my narcissist that I have a concealed weapon? I want to deter him.

Answer: My advice is to conceal the weapon both physically and verbally. For two reasons:

One, narcissists are paranoids. NPD is often co-morbid with PPD (Paranoid PD). The presence of a weapon confirms their worst persecutory delusions and often tips them over the edge.

The second reason has to do with the balance of power (or rather balance of terror) complex. In his mind, the narcissist is superior in every way. This fantasised and grandiose superiority is what maintains the precarious equilibrium of his personality.

A gun – the virile symbol that it is – upsets the power relations in favour of the victim. It is a humiliation, a failure, a mockery, a defying challenge. The narcissist will likely seek to restore the previous poise by 'diminishing' his opponent and 'containing' the menace. In other words, the presence of a gun guarantees conflict – and, as you said, a potentially lethal one. As the narcissist – now terrified by his own deranged persecutory phantasms – seeks redress, he may resort to the physical elimination of the source of his frustration (battering, or worse)."

Narcissists and Guns by - Sam Vaknin
http://www.narcissistic-abuse.com/9.html#Guns%20and%20Narcissists

"I loved her the way only a narcissist knows how to, the way a junkie loves his drugs."

Excerpts from the Archives of the Narcissism List - Part 29 - Sam Vaknin
http://samvak.tripod.com/archive29.html

"To obtain Narcissistic Supply, the narcissist has to toil. He has to work hard to create Sources of Supply (PNSS, SNSS) and to maintain them. These are demanding tasks. They are often very tiring."

Narcissistic Signal, Stimulus and Hibernation Mini-Cycles - Sam Vaknin
http://samvak.tripod.com/faq43.html

"Only when the narcissist goes through a massive life crisis (divorce, death in the family, near death experience, bankruptcy, incarceration, abuse, humiliation, exile, etc.) - only then does he begin to reflect on his life and on himself. But, even then, narcissists are interested in getting things 'back to how they were' - not in changing."

Ask Sam Vaknin
http://groups.msn.com/NARCISSISTICPERSONALITYDISORDER/general.msnw?action=get_message&mview=0&ID_Message=15404

"The word 'love' is understood by the narcissist to mean 'dependence', 'neediness', 'ability to provide Narcissistic Supply', 'becoming the narcissist's extension and property'. In these - distorted and sick - senses of the word, all narcissists love to be loved..."

Ask Sam Vaknin
http://groups.msn.com/NARCISSISTICPERSONALITYDISORDER/general.msnw?action=get_message&mview=0&ID_Message=15404

"Question: Yet, we often find that narcissists abandon their efforts in mid-stream, give up, vanish, lose interest, devalue former pursuits, or slump. Why is that?

Answer: A challenge, or even a guaranteed eventual triumph - are meaningless in the absence of onlookers. The narcissist needs an audience to applaud, affirm, recoil, approve, admire, adore, fear, or even detest him. He craves the attention and depends on the Narcissistic Supply only others can provide. The narcissist derives sustenance only from the outside - his emotional innards are hollow and moribund."

Ask Sam Vaknin
http://groups.msn.com/NARCISSISTICPERSONALITYDISORDER/general.msnw?action=get_message&mview=0&ID_Message=15404

"Narcissists are incapable of introspection. This inability to 'watch themselves from the outside' is what often gets them into trouble."

Ask Sam Vaknin
http://groups.msn.com/NARCISSISTICPERSONALITYDISORDER/general.msnw?action=get_message&mview=0&ID_Message=15404

"Whether he contacts you again or not also depends on whether he found a substitute Source of Narcissistic Supply and on whether he thinks that you could supply him in future, even as an auxilliary, 'reserve'."

Ask Sam Vaknin
http://groups.msn.com/NARCISSISTICPERSONALITYDISORDER/general.msnw?action=get_message&mview=0&ID_Message=15404

"Withholding (the silent treatment), countering (refuting or invalidating the spouse's statements or actions), discounting (putting down her emotions, possessions, experiences, hopes, and fears), sadistic and brutal humour, blocking (avoiding a meaningful exchange, diverting the conversation, changing the subject), blaming and accusing, judging and criticising, undermining and sabotaging, threatening, name calling, forgetting and denying, ordering around, denial, and abusive anger."

The Mind of the Abuser - Sam Vaknin
http://www.suite101.com/article.cfm/18046/101757

"Successful narcissists are frequently targeted by stalkers and erotomaniacs – usually mentally ill people who develop a fixation of a sexual and emotional nature on the narcissist. When inevitably rebuffed, they become vindictive and even violent."

Abusing the Gullible Narcissist - Sam Vaknin
http://www.suite101.com/article.cfm/6514/101693

"Paradoxically, the narcissist does not mind being humiliated if this were to make him more unique. For instance: if the injustice involved in the process of humiliation is unprecedented, or if the humiliating acts or words place the narcissist in a unique position – he often tries to encourage such behaviours and elicit them from his human environment. In this case, he fantasises how he demeans and debases his opponents by forcing them to behave even more barbarously than usual, so that their unjust deeds will be universally recognised as such and condemned and the narcissist be publicly vindicated. In short: martyrdom is as good a method of obtaining Narcissist Supply as any."

Abusing the Gullible Narcissist - Sam Vaknin
http://www.suite101.com/article.cfm/6514/101693

"Fantasy, though, has its limits and once reached, the narcissist is likely to experience a wave of self-hatred and self-loathing. These are a result of feeling helpless and of realising the depths of his dependence on Narcissistic Supply. These feelings culminate in severe self-directed aggression: depression, destructive, self-defeating or suicidal ideation. These reactions, inevitably and naturally, terrify the narcissist. He tries to project them on to his environment. The way from this defence mechanism to an obsessive-compulsive disorder or even to a psychotic episode is short. The narcissist is suddenly besieged by disturbing, uncontrollable thoughts whose violence cannot be harnessed. He develops ritualistic reactions to them: a sequence of motions, an act, or an obsessive counter-thought. Or he might visualise his aggression, or experience auditory hallucinations. Humiliation affects the narcissist this deeply."

Abusing the Narcissist - Sam Vaknin
http://www.suite101.com/article.cfm/6514/101693

"There is no 'typical victim'. Women in all walks of life, wealthy and poor, smart and dumb, tall and short, head turning and less so – all fall prey to abuse."

Ask Sam Vaknin
http://groups.msn.com/NARCISSISTICPERSONALITYDISORDER/general.msnw?action=get_message&mview=0&ID_Message=15404

"He is as immature and infantile as a child. How many times have you told your child 'white lies' to motivate her to do something or to refrain from doing something? One caveat, though: Do NOT make specific promises. These will come back to haunt you and may provoke aggression if not fulfilled."

Ask Sam Vaknin
http://groups.msn.com/NARCISSISTICPERSONALITYDISORDER/general.msnw?action=get_message&mview=0&ID_Message=15404

"The typical narcissist has a short attention span and believes that the world is a random, menacing place. Catch as catch can. Carpe Diem (seize the day). The narcissist lurches at any potential source with a 'charm attack' that often, alas, proves irresistible. Very few narcissists are sufficiently cold and calculated to cultivate long-term Sources of Supply. It's now or never."

Ask Sam Vaknin

http://groups.msn.com/NARCISSISTICPERSONALITYDISORDER/general.msnw?action=get_message&mview=0&ID_Message=15404

"Question: I would like to know exactly what our N's were thinking when they first met us. Did they look at us and think 'Ah, she looks like a good target, I'll try this one and see what happens, lets see what I can get out of her, what can she give me, what can she do for me'.

Answer: Pathological narcissism - the addiction to and pursuit of Narcissistic Supply to regulate a labile sense of self-worth - is not a conscious CHOICE, or a lifestyle, or a profession. It is the quiddity (the essence) of the narcissist. Do bees plan to sting? Do tigers analyse their hunting patterns? Do mothers love their children by design? It just comes to the narcissist naturally. I see a beautiful woman, who is also reasonably clever - and I want to 'convert' her, to make her admire me, to cause her to spread news and views about me and 'proselytise' to ever expanding concentric circles of family and friends. This wish is the psychological equivalent of hunger or thirst (or sex drive). It is a craving gradually translated into a plan of action. But first comes the insatiable addiction to Narcissistic Supply - and only then a cognitive 'blueprint' of hunting, conversion and conquest."

Ask Sam Vaknin

http://groups.msn.com/NARCISSISTICPERSONALITYDISORDER/general.msnw?action=get_message&mview=0&ID_Message=15404

"Closure
Everyone learns from experience. The question is what is learned. The narcissist has alloplastic defences. In other words, he tends to blame the world for failures, mishaps, problems, and defeats. Because he has a preconceived notion of a hostile, menacing Universe - his experience only serves to fortify his prejudices. The narcissist learns nothing, forgets nothing, and

forgives nothing. A post-mortem of a relationship conducted with a narcissist is very frustrating because it never achieves closure. The narcissist is interested exclusively in allocating blame and generating guilt – not in progressing, developing, atoning, soothing, or concluding anything. Such exercises in futility are best avoided."

Excerpts from the Archives of the Narcissism List - Part 43 - Sam Vaknin
http://samvak.tripod.com/archive43.html
The Three Forms of Closure - Sam Vaknin
http://samvak.tripod.com/abuse17.html

"The Silent Treatment
Resuming the conversation as though nothing happened is due to the internal needs of the narcissist and especially his need for renewed Narcissistic Supply. Being a control freak, the narcissist determines the timing of everything: when to have sex, when to talk, when to go on a vacation, etc. You have no right to retaliate for his behaviour because you do not exist as a separate entity with your own views, boundaries, emotions and needs. At best the narcissist considers you a wayward child in need of disciplining. At worst, you are no more than an implement, or an extension of the narcissist. Silent treatment is meted out by children and narcissists – treat the latter as you would the former."

What is Abuse? - Sam Vaknin
http://samvak.tripod.com/abuse.html

"Paraphilias (sexual deviance) are very common among narcissists and, more so, among psychopaths. (They) usually reflect an utter inability to recognise other people's boundaries by seeking to merge with them and thus control them. The narcissistic psychopath also expresses his auto-eroticism (self-infatuation) in group sex, homosexuality, or incest. Hence, the psychopath's need to idealise you – in effect, he is idealising and idolising himself."

Excerpts from the Archives of the Narcissism List - Sam Vaknin
http://www.narcissistic-abuse.com/archive01.html

"Unfortunately, I do not think you have seen the last of him. As far as he is concerned, he 'owns' you – you are his property to do with as he pleases when he pleases. You are an extension of his Self. There is no telling or predicting when he will resurface – but, most likely, when you find happiness: a new mate, a new job, a new friend.

Bear this in mind. Tell everyone you can trust about what had happened. Inform local law enforcement officers. Take precautionary measures – though there is no need to panic or become paranoid. Psychopaths rarely act out of passion and suddenly. They are very cold and calculated and you are likely to receive many warning signs before danger becomes real."

Excerpts from the Archives of the Narcissism List - Sam Vaknin
http://www.narcissistic-abuse.com/archive01.html

"Impregnating the woman is a classic method of 'controlling' and 'binding' her down. The narcissistic psychopath aware of the shallowness and transience of his own simulated emotions – attributed the same fleetingness to his partner. Saddled with a baby, she is unlikely to vanish on him."

Excerpts from the Archives of the Narcissism List - Sam Vaknin
http://www.narcissistic-abuse.com/archive01.html

"Narcissistic psychopaths have no friends, or lovers, or spouses, or children, or family – they have only objects to be manipulated. Narcissists have a problem perceiving other people's ability to conceive of ideas, to have their own needs, emotions, and preference. Wouldn't you be startled if your television set suddenly informed you that it would rather not work on a Sunday? Or if your vacuum cleaner wanted to befriend you? To narcissists, other people are instruments, tools, sources – in short: objects. Objects are not supposed to have opinions or to make independent choices and decisions – especially if they don't comply with the narcissist's worldview, plans, or if they do not cater to his needs.

1. They feel bad – so bad, in effect that it prompts them either to coerce you back into an imagined relationship (stalking) – or to delete you altogether from their mind and history (discard and devalue). This is called narcissistic injury or narcissistic wound.
2. Compelled by their addiction – by the inexorable need to regulate their labile sense of self-worth – narcissists cannot remain for long without Sources of Narcissistic Supply. So, yes, they move on to the next source in lightning speed.

But narcissists/psychopaths rarely abandon a Source of Supply. She may be keeping you on ice, part of her 'stable', a reserve – and will re-emerge when she is in need of a dose of Narcissistic Supply and all other sources have been depleted."

>
> Adolescent Narcissist - A Case Study - Sam Vaknin
> http://samvak.tripod.com/faq16.html

"Freedom03: I would like to know if the narcissist is aware of what they are doing?

Vaknin: Aware, cunning, premeditated, and, sometimes, even enjoying every bit of it. But it is not malice that drives them. They believe in their own destiny, superiority, entitlement, exemption from laws promulgated by mere mortals."

> Relationships with Abusive Narcissists Online Chat Transcript
> http://healthyplace.com/communities/personality_disorders/site/Transcripts/abusive_narcissists.htm

"Sometimes it looks hopeless. Abusers are ruthless, immoral, sadistic, calculated, cunning, persuasive, deceitful – in short, they appear to be invincible. They easily sway the system in their favour. Here is a list of escalating countermeasures. They represent the distilled experience of thousands of victims of abuse. They may help you cope with abuse and overcome it."

> Coping with Your Abuser - Sam Vaknin
> http://samvak.tripod.com/abuse3.html

"Do not talk to him on the phone. Hang up the minute you hear his voice."

> Coping with Your Abuser - Sam Vaknin
> http://samvak.tripod.com/abuse3.html

"Abusers are predators, attuned to the subtlest emotional cues of their prey. Never show your abuser that you are afraid or that you are less than resolute. The willingness to negotiate is perceived as a weakness by bullies. Violent offenders are insatiable. Do not succumb to blackmail or emotional extortion – once you start compromising, you won't see the end of it."

> Avoiding Your Abuser - II. The Conflictive Posture - Sam Vaknin
> http://samvak.tripod.com/abuse6.html

"Trap your abuser. Treat him as he treats you. Involve others. Bring it into the open. Nothing like sunshine to disinfect abuse."

> Coping with Your Abuser - Sam Vaknin
> http://samvak.tripod.com/abuse3.html

"I love him. I cannot leave him like that. He is like a crippled small child. My heart goes out to him. Will he ever get better? Can he ever get better?"

> Can the Narcissist Get Better? - Sam Vaknin
> http://samvak.tripod.com/10.html

"Narcissists sniff other people's emotions the way hound dogs sniff blood."

> Ask Sam Vaknin
> http://groups.msn.com/NARCISSISTICPERSONALITYDISORDER/general.msnw?action=get_message&mview=0&ID_Message=15404

"His bouts of periodic generosity have nothing whatsoever to do with you. Whenever he needs to fine tune his wavering sense of self-worth and to buttress his self-image as a giving, caring, and kind person - he is out to buy you a new carpet. You are Sources of Secondary Narcissistic Supply - mute witnesses to his largesse and big-heartedness. You are nothing more than that - the human equivalents of tape recorders. The sole justification for your existence is to attest to his magnanimity. Hence also his disappearances (when supply is plentiful). Exasperating, isn't it?"

> Ask Sam Vaknin
> http://groups.msn.com/NARCISSISTICPERSONALITYDISORDER/general.msnw?action=get_message&mview=0&ID_Message=15404

"Narcissists are concerned with the happiness of their nearest and dearest only insofar as it prevents the loss of a Source of Supply. A married narcissist tries to make his spouse happy as long as she serves as a good fount of adulation, admiration, attention, approval, and affirmation. If she is unhappy - she walks. If she is happy - she stays. Think of it as a maintenance chore: You service your car. If you don't maintain it - is stops. You maintain it - it gets you places. The irony is that narcissists - being emotional aliens - don't know what makes people tick (they lack empathy). So, they get it all wrong. Their efforts to secure the happiness of their Sources of Supply backfire and lead to unhappiness and abandonment."

Ask Sam Vaknin
http://groups.msn.com/NARCISSISTICPERSONALITYDISORDER/general.msnw?action=get_message&mview=0&ID_Message=15404

"Narcissists are compulsively competitive because their grandiose fantasies are unrealistic and unattainable. They must have the last word and the upper hand – or risk experiencing the excruciating Grandiosity Gap (the abyss between reality and the False Self-image). Emotionally, they cannot afford to be 'defeated' and thus 'humiliated'. Too much rides on it – the very precarious balance of their personality."

Ask Sam Vaknin
http://groups.msn.com/NARCISSISTICPERSONALITYDISORDER/general.msnw?action=get_message&mview=0&ID_Message=15404

"Living with a narcissist is a harrowing experience. It can tilt one's mind toward abnormal reactions (really normal reactions to an abnormal situation)."

Narcissists, Paranoiacs and Psychotherapists - Sam Vaknin
http://samvak.tripod.com/faq26to27.html

"Arguably the most hurtful thing about a relationship with a narcissist is the ultimate realisation of how interchangeable one is, as far as the narcissist is concerned."

Narcissists, Paranoiacs and Psychotherapists - Sam Vaknin
http://samvak.tripod.com/faq26to27.html

"The Grandiosity Hangover and the Grandiosity Gap are the two major vulnerabilities of the narcissist."

Grandiosity Hangover and Narcissistic Baiting - Sam Vaknin
http://samvak.tripod.com/journal56.html

"Such a narcissist reacts with alarm and rage to any sign of independence and autonomy in his 'charges'. He tries to 'freeze' everyone around him in their 'allocated' positions and 'assigned roles'. His world is rigid and immovable, predictable and static, fully under his control. He punishes for 'transgressions' against this ordained order. He thus stifles life as a dynamic process of compromising and growing - rendering it instead a mere theatre, a tableau vivant."

The Two Loves of the Narcissist - Sam Vaknin
http://www.suite101.com/article.cfm/npd/102824

"The narcissist is egotistically committed only to his own well-being. To him, the objects of his 'love' are interchangeable and lowly. He idealises not because he is smitten by emotion - and discards and devalues similarly cold-bloodedly. A predator, always on the lookout, he debases the coin of 'love' as he corrupts everything else in himself and around him."

The Two Loves of the Narcissist - Sam Vaknin
http://www.suite101.com/article.cfm/npd/102824

"Women possess things that the narcissist needs. They have the biologically compatible equipment for sex. They provide emotional comfort through their friendship and love. This kind of emotional resonance is not available from any other source."

The Concept of Narcissistic Supply - Sam Vaknin
http://samvak.tripod.com/msla6.html

"They are said to be in love with themselves. But this is a fallacy. Narcissus is not in love with HIMSELF. He is in love with his REFLECTION. There is a major difference between True Self and reflected-self."

The Soul of the Narcissist - Sam Vaknin
http://www.narcissistic-abuse.com/msla.html

"Moreover, to satisfy his need of women, the narcissist has to convince them to be with him. In other words, he has to promote himself and to win them over. This casts women as judges. They are granted the power to compare, evaluate, rate, adjudicate, accept, reject, or abandon. They possess the capacity to hurt the narcissist by rejecting him or by abandoning him - and he feels that they flaunt this power. This realisation cannot coexist with a feeling of omnipotence. To restore the proper balance of power, the narcissist must frustrate women. He must re-acquire his superior position of judgement and decision-making. Women are anti-narcissistic agents. They are perceived by the narcissist to have an all-pervading, all-penetrating 'X-rays' look, the kind that might reach the narcissist's TRUE Self. This is a real threat. These ominous supernatural capacities evoke strong emotional reactions in the narcissist."

The Concept of Narcissistic Supply - Sam Vaknin
http://samvak.tripod.com/msla6.html

"Question: An adult narcissist, in other words, is still stuck in his 'terrible twos' and is possessed with the emotional maturity of a toddler. Does the narcissist want to be liked?

Answer: Would you wish to be liked by your television set? To the narcissist, people are mere tools, Sources of Supply. If he must be liked by them in order to secure this supply - he strives to make sure they like him. If he can only be feared - he makes sure they fear him. He does not really care either way as long as he is being attended to. Attention - whether in the form of fame or infamy - is what it's all about. His world revolves around his constant mirroring. I am seen therefore I exist, sayeth the narcissist.

Additionally, narcissists get tired of their sources. There is no mathematical formula, which governs this. It depends on numerous variables. Usually, the relationship lasts until the narcissist 'gets used' to the source and its stimulating effects wear off OR until a better Source of Supply presents itself."

Ask Sam Vaknin
http://groups.msn.com/NARCISSISTICPERSONALITYDISORDER/general.msnw?action=get_message&mview=0&ID_Message=15404
http://groups.msn.com/PSYCHOPATH/general.msnw?action=get_message&mview=0&ID_Message=9350

"The narcissist often strikes people are 'laid back' - or, less charitably: lazy, parasitic, spoiled, and self-indulgent. But, as usual with narcissists, appearances deceive. Narcissists are either compulsively driven over-achievers - or chronic under-achieving wastrels."

Whistling in the Dark - Sam Vaknin
http://samvak.tripod.com/journal58.html

"The abused are often on the verge of a nervous breakdown: harassed, unkempt, irritable, impatient, abrasive, and hysterical. Confronted with this contrast between a polished, self-controlled, and suave abuser and his harried casualties – it is easy to reach the conclusion that the real victim is the abuser, or that both parties abuse each other equally. The prey's acts of self-defence, assertiveness, or insistence on her rights are interpreted as aggression."

Pathologising the Victim – Sam Vaknin
(from "Toxic Relationships – Abuse and its Aftermath", 2004)
http://groups.msn.com/NARCISSISTICPERSONALITYDISORDER/toxicrelationshipspathologizingthevictim.msnw

"Better to play ball and adopt the sleek mannerisms of your abuser. Sadly, sometimes the only way to convince your therapist that it is not all in your head and that you are a victim – is by being insincere and by staging a well-calibrated performance, replete with the correct vocabulary. Therapists have Pavlovian reactions to certain phrases and theories and to certain 'presenting signs and symptoms' (behaviours during the first few sessions). Learn these – and use them to your advantage. It is your only chance."

Pathologising the Victim – Sam Vaknin
(from "Toxic Relationships – Abuse and its Aftermath", 2004)
http://groups.msn.com/NARCISSISTICPERSONALITYDISORDER/toxicrelationshipspathologizingthevictim.msnw

"When his sources become weary, rebellious, tired, bored, disgusted, repelled, or plainly amused by the narcissist's incessant dependence, his childish craving for attention, his exaggerated or even paranoid fears which lead to obsessive-compulsive behaviours, and his 'drama queen' temper tantrums – he resorts to emotional extortion, straight blackmail, abuse, or misuse of his authority, and criminal or antisocial conduct. If these fail, the narcissist devalues and discards the very people he so idealised and cherished only a short while before.

Nor is the narcissist deterred by possible punishment or regards himself subject to Man-made laws. His sense of entitlement coupled with the conviction of his own superiority lead him to believe in his invincibility, invulnerability, immunity, and divinity. The narcissist holds human edicts, rules, and regulations in disdain and human penalties in disdain. He regards human needs and emotions as weaknesses to be predatorily exploited."

The Professions of the Narcissist - Sam Vaknin
http://www.suite101.com/article.cfm/npd/103814

"Choosing to live with an abuser is like opting to share a cage with a predator. No matter how domesticated, Nature is bound to prevail. You are more likely than not to end up as the abuser's next meal."

Avoiding the Abuser - I. The Submissive Posture - Sam Vaknin
http://www.suite101.com/article.cfm/9128/103326

"To your abuser, you are an object, no matter how ostensibly revered and cherished. Hence the battering. He monopolises your time and your mind. He makes for you even the minutest choices: what to wear, what to cook for dinner, when to go out and with whom. In extreme cases, he regards even your body as his to share with others, if he sees fit."

Avoiding the Abuser - I. The Submissive Posture - Sam Vaknin
http://www.suite101.com/article.cfm/9128/103326

"Primary Narcissistic Supply (PNS) is ANY kind of NS provided by others who are not 'meaningful' or 'significant' others. Adulation, attention, affirmation, fame, notoriety, sexual conquests - are all forms of PNS. Secondary NS (SNS) emanates from people who are in CONSTANT, repetitive or continuous touch with the narcissist. It includes the important roles of Narcissistic Accumulation and Narcissistic Regulation, among others."

Narcissists and Women- - Sam Vaknin
http://samvak.tripod.com/faq79.html

"What does 'pain' mean to narcissists? Do they feel pain emotionally? When I use terms like 'pain' and 'envy', they mean normal feelings of pain and envy.

Narcissists feel negative emotions as all others do. They suppress only their positive emotions and replace them with false substitutes (Narcissistic Supply instead of love, for instance).

Narcissists are pompous, grandiose, repulsive and contradictory. There is a serious mismatch between who they really are and what they really achieve – and how they feel about themselves. It is not that the narcissist merely THINKS that he is far superior to other humans intellectually. The perception of his superiority is ingrained in him, it is a part of his every mental cell, an all-pervasive sensation, an instinct and a drive. He feels that he is entitled to special treatment and to outstanding consideration because he is such a unique specimen. He knows this to be true – the same way one knows that one is surrounded by air."

> Do Narcissists Have Emotions? - Sam Vaknin
> http://www.narcissistic-abuse.com/faq33.html

"The narcissist feels entitled to and deserving of ever increasing amounts of Narcissistic Supply. Narcissism is a drug addiction: as doses consumed increase – the impact (elation, 'happiness') decreases. The addict needs progressively more to maintain his high. Additionally, it is not realistic to expect the narcissist never to encounter disagreement or criticism. Hence, narcissistic rage and abusive behaviours are inevitable."

> Ask Sam Vaknin
> http://groups.msn.com/NARCISSISTICPERSONALITYDISORDER/general.msnw?action=get_message&mview=0&ID_Message=15404

"Don't make excuses for him. Don't try to understand him. Do not empathise with him – he, surely, does not empathise with you. He has no mercy on you – you, in return, do not harbour misplaced pity for him. Never give him a second chance. React with your full arsenal to the first transgression. Teach him a lesson he is unlikely to forget. Make him go elsewhere for his sadistic pursuits or to offload his frustrations."

> Avoiding the Abuser II - The Conflictive Posture - Sam Vaknin
> http://www.suite101.com/article.cfm/9128/103895

"Thus, the complaints of a victim are likely to be met with hostility and suspicion by the offender's parents or siblings, for instance. Instead of reining in the abusive conduct, they are likely to pathologise the victim ('She is a nutcase') or label her ('She is a whore or a bitch'). Nor is the victim of abuse likely to fare better in the hands of law enforcement agencies, the courts, counselours, therapists, and guardians ad litem. The propensity of these institutions is to assume that the abused has a hidden agenda - to abscond with her husband's property, or to deny him custody or visitation rights."

> Reforming the Abuser - Sam Vaknin
> http://www.suite101.com/article.cfm/18046/104000

"How to get your abuser to see reason in the first place? How to obtain for him the help he needs - without involving law enforcement agencies, the authorities, or the courts? Any attempt to broach the subject of the abuser's mental problems frequently ends in harangues and worse. It is positively dangerous to mention the abuser's shortcomings or imperfections to his face."

> Reforming the Abuser - Sam Vaknin
> http://samvak.tripod.com/abusefamily6.html

"Personal boundaries are not negotiable, neither can they be determined from the outside. Your abusive bully should have no say in setting them or in upholding them. Only you decide when they have been breached, what constitutes a transgression, what is excusable and what not."

> Reforming the Abuser - Sam Vaknin
> http://www.suite101.com/article.cfm/18046/104000

"Ask him to define - preferably in writing - what he expects from you and where he thinks that you, or your 'performance' are 'deficient'. Try to accommodate his reasonable demands and ignore the rest. Do not, at this stage, present a counter-list. This will come later. To move him to attend couple or marital therapy, tell him that you need his help to restore your relationship to its former warmth and intimacy. Admit to faults of your own which you want 'fixed' so as to be a better mate. Appeal to his narcissism and self-image as the omnipotent and omniscient macho. Humour him for a while."

> Contracting With Your Abuser - Sam Vaknin
> http://www.suite101.com/article.cfm/18046/104159

"Imagine a first or second date. You can already tell if he is a would-be abuser."

> How to Spot an Abuser on Your First Date? - Sam Vaknin
> http://www.suite101.com/article.cfm/9128/104161

"The narcissist analyses (and internalises) everything in terms of blame and guilt, superiority and inferiority, gain (victory) and loss (defeat) and the resulting matrix of Narcissistic Supply. Narcissists are binary contraptions. Thus, the formula is very simple:

Shift the blame to yourself ('I don't know what happened to me, I have changed, it is my fault, I am to blame for this, you are constant, reliable and consistent').

Tell him you feel guilty (excruciatingly so, in great and picturesque detail).

Tell him how superior he is and how inferior you feel. Make this separation your loss and his absolute, unmitigated gain.

Convince him that he is likely to gain more supply from others (future women?) than he ever did or will from you.

BUT

Make clear that your decision – though evidently 'erroneous' and 'pathological' – is FINAL, irrevocable and that all contact is to be severed henceforth.

And never leave ANYTHING in writing."

Excerpts from the Archives of the Narcissism List - Part 35 - Sam Vaknin
http://samvak.tripod.com/archive35.html

"I make a point of saying ... that the invert must be or become emotionally and financially independent (if you don't do this he will eat you up and when he has finished with you and you are nothing but a husk, you will be expelled from his life in one big vomit). It is really important for you to start to take responsibility for your own emotional wellness without regard to how he treats you. Remember that the narcissist has the emotional maturity of a two-year old! Don't expect much in the way of emotional depth or support in your relationship – he simply is not capable of anything that sophisticated."

The Inverted Narcissist - Sam Vaknin
http://samvak.tripod.com/faq66.html

"Bipolar patients in the manic phase exhibit many of the signs and symptoms of pathological narcissism – hyperactivity, self-centredness, lack of empathy, and control freakery. During this recurring chapter of the disease, the patient is euphoric, has grandiose fantasies, spins unrealistic schemes, and has frequent rage attacks (is irritable) if her or his wishes and plans are (inevitably) frustrated."

Misdiagnosing Narcissism - The Bipolar I Disorder - Sam Vaknin
http://samvak.tripod.com/journal71.html

"The Bipolar's swollen self-esteem, overstated self-confidence, obvious grandiosity, and delusional fantasies are akin to the narcissist's and are the source of the diagnostic confusion."

Misdiagnosing Narcissism - The Bipolar I Disorder - Sam Vaknin
http://samvak.tripod.com/journal71.html
Misdiagnosing Narcissism - Asperger's Disorder - Sam Vaknin
http://samvak.tripod.com/journal72.html
Misdiagnosing Narcissism - Generalised Anxiety Disorder (GAD) - Sam Vaknin
http://samvak.tripod.com/journal93.html

"One should not romanticise the narcissist. His regrets are forever linked to his fears of losing his sources. His loneliness vanishes when he is awash with Narcissistic Supply. Narcissists have no enemies. They have only Sources of Narcissistic Supply. An enemy means attention means supply. One holds sway over one's enemy. If the narcissist has the power to provoke emotions in you – you are still a Source of Supply, regardless of WHICH emotions these are. He seeks you out probably because he has absolutely no other NS Sources at this stage. Narcissists frantically try to recycle their old and wasted sources in such a situation. But he would NOT have done even this had he not felt that he could still successfully extract a modicum of NS from you (even to attack someone is to recognise his existence and to attend to him!!!). So, what should you do?"

Excerpts from the Archives of the Narcissism List - Part 10 - Sam Vaknin
http://samvak.tripod.com/archive10.html

"The more helpless the woman – the more dependent she is on the narcissist and the better Source of Secondary Supply she becomes. Narcissists avoid autonomous, strong-minded, accomplished women (unless they can play on their emotional vulnerabilities)."

Ask Sam Vaknin
http://groups.msn.com/NARCISSISTICPERSONALITYDISORDER/general.msnw?action=get_message&mview=0&ID_Message=15404

"Why don't you just say 'good riddance' and throw a party?"

Ask Sam Vaknin
http://groups.msn.com/NARCISSISTICPERSONALITYDISORDER/general.msnw?action=get_message&mview=0&ID_Message=15404

"Question: He has been violent toward me and (our pets). Now that I am held in the completely devalued and dehumanised role by him, he is menacing me every time he sees me. In the last week he has said to me, rather matter-of fact: (1) 'You know I'll probably kill you one day', (2) 'You might be found in a dumpster one day', (3) 'You deserve to be punched in the face', and (4) 'I'd like to hit you in the head and hear something crack'. My question is, how likely is he to carry out his homicidal ideations.

Answer: Get out of there and do it fast and comprehensively. And take his threats very seriously, is my insight, comment, and advice, rolled into one."

Ask Sam Vaknin
http://groups.msn.com/NARCISSISTICPERSONALITYDISORDER/general.msnw?action=get_message&mview=0&ID_Message=15404

"Verbalise your emotions, needs, preferences, and choices without aggression but with assertiveness and determination. Some abusers – the narcissistic ones – are detached from reality. They avoid it actively and live in fantasies of everlasting and unconditional love. They refuse to accept the inevitable consequences of their own actions. It is up to you to correct these cognitive and emotional deficits. You may encounter opposition – even violence – but, in the long-run, facing reality pays."

Reforming the Abuser – Sam Vaknin
http://samvak.tripod.com/abusefamily6.html

"The abuser is constantly on the lookout for a weakening of your resolve. He is repeatedly testing your mettle and resilience. He pounces on any and every vulnerability, uncertainty, or hesitation. Don't give him these chances."

Reforming the Abuser – Sam Vaknin
http://samvak.tripod.com/abusefamily6.html

"It is not so easy to get the narcissist out of your system. He is a master at playing on your vulnerabilities, penetrating your defences, and lodging himself as a voice in your tortured brain."

Ask Sam Vaknin
http://groups.msn.com/NARCISSISTICPERSONALITYDISORDER/general.msnw?action=get_message&mview=0&ID_Message=15404

"Question: I have a psych evaluations of my XNH. There is a line in the one of the evaluations that says he displays 'resilient narcissism'. What does it mean?

Answer: 'Resilient' means intractable, untreatable, beyond intervention, exacerbated, aggravated. In short: very bad and beyond help."

Ask Sam Vaknin
http://groups.msn.com/NARCISSISTICPERSONALITYDISORDER/general.msnw?action=get_message&mview=0&ID_Message=15404

"The cerebral narcissist is competitive and intolerant of criticism or disagreement. The subjugation and subordination of others demand the establishment of his undisputed intellectual superiority or professional authority. Alexander Lowen has an excellent exposition of this 'hidden or tacit competition'. The cerebral narcissist aspires to perfection. Thus, even the slightest and most inconsequential challenge to his authority is inflated by him. Hence, the disproportionateness of his reactions."

Narcissists, Disagreements and Criticism - Sam Vaknin
http://samvak.tripod.com/faq73.html

"Psychopaths have alloplastic defences. They blame others for their mishaps and failures. You are the focus of his frustration and aggression. If hurting you requires hurting your children – he wouldn't think twice."

Ask Sam Vaknin
http://groups.msn.com/NARCISSISTICPERSONALITYDISORDER/general.msnw?action=get_message&mview=0&ID_Message=15404

"Question: His father is a narcissist. We divorced a few months ago, but he has visitation rights. You wrote that 'narcissism breeds narcissism'. How can I prevent my child from becoming a narcissist under his father's influence?

Answer: The only thing you can do to prevent your son from emulating his father - is to present to him another role model of a NON-narcissist - YOU. Hopefully, when he grows up, he will prefer your model to his father's. But there is only that much you can do. You cannot control the developmental path of your son. Exerting unlimited control over your son is what narcissism is all about - and is exactly what you should avoid at all costs, however worried you might be."

How Can I Save My Child? - Sam Vaknin
http://samvak.tripod.com/4.html

"The narcissistic parent regards his or her child as a multi-faceted Source of Narcissistic Supply."

Narcissistic Parents - Sam Vaknin
http://samvak.tripod.com/faq5.html

"From the first moments of an encounter with another person, the abuser is on the prowl. He collects information. The more he knows about his potential victim - the better able he is to coerce, manipulate, charm, extort or convert it 'to the cause'. The abuser does not hesitate to misuse the information he gleans, regardless of its intimate nature or the circumstances in which he obtained it. This is a powerful tool in his armoury."

Ambient Abuse - Sam Vaknin
http://samvak.tripod.com/abuse10.html

"The abuser tends to be comfortable lying, having years of practice, and so can sound believable when making baseless statements. The abuser benefits ... when professionals believe that they can 'just tell' who is lying and who is telling the truth, and so fail to adequately investigate."

Conning the System - Sam Vaknin
http://samvak.tripod.com/abusefamily10.html

"The narcissistic shame - which is the experience of the Grandiosity Gap (and its affective correlate). Subjectively it is experienced as a pervasive feeling of worthlessness (the regulation of self-worth is the crux of pathological narcissism), 'invisibleness' and ridiculousness. The patient feels pathetic and foolish, deserving of mockery and humiliation. Narcissists adopt all kinds of defences to counter narcissistic shame. They develop addictive or impulsive behaviours. They deny, withdraw, rage, engage in the compulsive pursuit of some kind of (unattainable, of course) perfection. They display haughtiness and exhibitionism and so on. All these defences are employed primitively (or are primitive, like splitting) and involve Projective Identification."

>   Can the Narcissist Have a Meaningful Life? - Sam Vaknin
>   http://samvak.tripod.com/faq01.html

"The narcissist differs from normal people in that his is a HIGHLY unrealistic personal narrative."

>   Can the Narcissist Have a Meaningful Life? - Sam Vaknin
>   http://samvak.tripod.com/faq01.html

"Abuse is the ultimate act of perverted intimacy. The abuser invades the victim's body, pervades his psyche, and possesses his mind. Deprived of contact with others and starved for human interactions, the prey bonds with the predator. 'Traumatic bonding', akin to the Stockholm Syndrome, is about hope and the search for meaning in the brutal and indifferent and nightmarish Universe of the abusive relationship. The abuser becomes the black hole at the centre of the victim's surrealistic galaxy, sucking in the sufferer's universal need for solace. The victim tries to 'control' his tormentor by becoming one with him (introjecting him) and by appealing to the monster's presumably dormant humanity and empathy."

>   The Narcissist - From Abuse to Suicide - Sam Vaknin
>   http://www.narcissistic-abuse.com/journal76.html

"The victims, on their part, do not believe that it is possible to effectively communicate to 'outsiders' what they have been through. The abuse seems to have occurred on 'another galaxy'."

>   The Narcissist - From Abuse to Suicide - Sam Vaknin
>   http://www.narcissistic-abuse.com/journal76.html

"Do not succumb to your weakness. It is tough living alone. You are bound to miss him horribly at times, selectively recalling only the good moments and the affection in your doomed relationship. Do not 'dip' into the poisonous offerings of your abuser. Do not relapse. Be strong. Fill your life with new hobbies, new interests, new friends, new loves, and a new purpose."

Interacting with Your Abuser - Sam Vaknin
http://samvak.tripod.com/abusefamily13.html

"Your abusive ex-partner will try to dazzle you with attention. Return all gifts he sends you – unopened and unacknowledged. Keep your communications with him to the bare, cold, minimum. Do not be impolite or abusive – it is precisely how he wants you to behave. It may be used against you in a court of law. Keep your cool but be firm."

Interacting with Your Abuser - Sam Vaknin
http://samvak.tripod.com/abusefamily13.html

"The child should learn to say 'no' and to walk away from potentially compromising situations with the abusive parent. The child should be brought up not to feel guilty for protecting itself and for demanding his or her rights. Remember this: An abusive parent is dangerous to the child."

Tell Your Children the Truth - Sam Vaknin
http://samvak.tripod.com/abuse13.html

"If he perceives you as autonomous, dangerously independent, and capable of bailing out and abandoning him – the narcissist acts the part of the sensitive, loving, compassionate, and empathic counterpart. Narcissists respect strength, they are awed by it. As long as you maintain a 'no nonsense' attitude, placing the narcissist on probation, he is likely to behave himself. If, on the other hand, you have resumed contact because you have capitulated to his threats or because you are manifestly dependent on him financially or emotionally – the narcissist will pounce on your frailty and exploit your fragility to the maximum. Following a perfunctory honeymoon, he will immediately seek to control and abuse you."

Back to La-La Land - Sam Vaknin
http://www.narcissistic-abuse.com/journal78.html

"Relationships with narcissists peter out slowly and tortuously. Narcissists do not provide closure. They stalk. They cajole, beg, promise, persuade, and, ultimately, succeed in doing the impossible yet again: sweep you off your feet, though you know better than to succumb to their spurious and superficial charms. So, you go back to your 'relationship' and hope for a better ending. You walk on eggshells. You become the epitome of submissiveness, a perfect Source of Narcissistic Supply, the ideal mate or spouse or partner or colleague. You keep your fingers crossed. But how does the narcissist react to the resurrection of the bond?"

Back to La-La Land - Sam Vaknin
http://www.narcissistic-abuse.com/journal78.html

"A Source of Narcissistic Supply is rendered 'redundant' when the narcissist has found another Source of Supply. Once this happens, there is little the original - now redundant - source can do. Devaluation and being discarded is inevitable. This is because novelty and conquest are very important to the narcissist. They enhance his sense of omnipotence. He takes old sources for granted and the value he attaches to their Narcissistic Supply goes down with time."

Ask Sam Vaknin (Part II)
http://groups.msn.com/NARCISSISTICPERSONALITYDISORDER/general.msnw?action=get_message&mview=0&ID_Message=45353

"Why is it so important to you to label him? He has clearly been abusive. Isn't this sufficient grounds for decision-making, even without the psychobabble mumbo-jumbo?"

Ask Sam Vaknin (Part II)
http://groups.msn.com/NARCISSISTICPERSONALITYDISORDER/general.msnw?action=get_message&mview=0&ID_Message=45353

"You are weighing my offer and I am waiting for your answer with hushed endurance. The armchairs are soft, the lobby is luxurious, as befits five-star hotels. I am not tense. I have anticipated your response even before I made my move."

The Conman Cometh - Sam Vaknin
http://gorgelink.org/vaknin/conman-en.html

"I am a con man and you are my victim. The swindle is unfolding here and now, in this very atrium, amid all the extravagance. I am selling your soul and collecting the change. I am sharpened, like a raw nerve firing impulses to you, receiving yours, an electrical-chemical dialog, consisting of your smelly sweat, my scented exudation. I permeate your cracks. I broker an alliance with your fears, your pains, defence compensatory mechanisms. I know you. I've got to meld us into one."

The Conman Cometh - Sam Vaknin
http://gorgelink.org/vaknin/conman-en.html

"The narcissist feels entitled to special amenities and benefits not accorded the 'rank and file'. He expects to be waited on hand and foot, to make free use of everyone's money and dispose of their assets liberally, and to be cynically exempt from the rules that he himself established (if such violation is pleasurable or gainful). In extreme cases, the narcissist feels above the law - any kind of law. This grandiose and haughty conviction leads to criminal acts, incestuous or polygamous relationships, and recurrent friction with the authorities."

The Cult of the Narcissist - Sam Vaknin
http://www.narcissistic-abuse.com/journal79.html

"Each personality disorder has its own form of Narcissistic Supply: HPD (Histrionic PD) - sex, seduction, flirtation, romance, body; NPD (Narcissistic PD) - adulation, admiration; BPD (Borderline PD) - presence (they are terrified of abandonment); AsPD (Antisocial PD) - money, power, control, fun."

Other Personality Disorders - Sam Vaknin
http://www.narcissistic-abuse.com/faq15.html

"You should not trust indiscriminately. No one is completely trustworthy in all fields. Most often our disappointments stem from our inability to separate one area of life from another. A person could be sexually loyal - but utterly dangerous when it comes to money (for instance, a gambler). Or a good, reliable father - but a womaniser.

The narcissist is notorious for his low threshold of resistance to boredom. His behaviour is impulsive and his biography tumultuous precisely because of his need to introduce uncertainty and risk to what he regards as 'stagnation' or 'slow death' (i.e., routine). Most interactions in the workplace are part of the rut – and thus constitute a reminder of this routine – deflating the narcissist's grandiose fantasies. Narcissists feel suffocated by intimacy, or by the constant reminders of the REAL, nitty-gritty world. It reduces them, makes them realise the Grandiosity Gap (between their self-image and reality). It is a threat to the precarious balance of their personality structures (mostly 'false', that is, invented) and treated as such."

The Narcissist in the Workplace - Sam Vaknin
http://malignantselflove.tripod.com/faq81.html

"He then becomes a satyr (or a nymphomaniac): indiscriminately engages in sex with multiple partners. His sex partners are considered by him to be objects not of desire – but of Narcissistic Supply. It is through the processes of successful seduction and sexual conquest that the narcissist derives his badly needed narcissistic 'fix'. The narcissist is likely to perfect his techniques of courting and regard his sexual exploits as a form of art. He usually exposes this side of him – in great detail – to others, to an audience, expecting to win their approval and admiration. Because the Narcissistic Supply in his case resides in the act of conquest and (what he perceives to be) subordination – the narcissist is forced to move on and to switch and bewitch partners very often."

NPD Catechism - Sam Vaknin
http://www.narcissistic-abuse.com/case04.html

"Slowly, the realisation that it was all my fault, that I was sick and needed help penetrated the decades old defences that I erected around me. This book is the documentation of a road of self-discovery. It was a painful process, which led to nowhere. I am no different – and no healthier – today than I was when I wrote this book. My disorder is here to stay, the prognosis is poor and alarming."

Can the Narcissist Become Violent? - Sam Vaknin
http://samvak.tripod.com/9.html

"Remember that many interactions are initiated by your abusive ex in order to trap or intimidate you. Keep referring him to your lawyer regarding legal issues, to your accountant or financial advisor concerning money matters, and to therapists, psychologists, and counselours with regards to everything else (yourself and your common children). Abusers react badly to such treatment. Yours will try to manipulate you into unintended contact. Do not respond to his pleading, romantic, nostalgic, flattering, or threatening e-mail and snail mail messages. Keep records of such correspondence and make it immediately available to the courts, law enforcement agencies, court-mandated evaluators, guardians ad litem, therapists, marital counselours, child psychologist - and to your good friends. Keep him away by obtaining restraining orders and injunctions aplenty."

Interacting with Your Abuser - Sam Vaknin
http://samvak.tripod.com/abusefamily13.html

"He suddenly fancies himself an actor, a guru, a political activist, an entrepreneur, or an irresistible hunk. He modifies his behaviour to conform to these new functions. He gradually morphs into the fabricated character and 'becomes' the fictitious protagonist he has created. All the mechanisms of pathological narcissism are at work during the bubble phase. The narcissist idealises the situation, the other 'actors', and the environment. He tries to control and manipulate his milieu into buttressing his false notions and perceptions. Faced with an inevitable Grandiosity Gap, he becomes disillusioned and bitter and devalues and discards the people, places, and circumstances involved in the bubble."

Grandiosity Bubbles - Sam Vaknin
http://www.suite101.com/article.cfm/npd/109348

"Question: Why should the narcissist look for another Source of Supply if the current Source of Supply is available and always accepts him back?

Answer: Cultivating a Source of Secondary Narcissistic Supply is a VERY time consuming and energy depleting affair. The narcissist always prefers the path of least resistance (reverting to old sources). The old source has the advantage of having witnessed and 'recorded' the narcissist's past grandeur. Her very repeated 'surrender' and 'yielding to his charm' IS the Narcissistic Supply he seeks."

Ask Sam Vaknin (Part II)
http://groups.msn.com/NARCISSISTICPERSONALITYDISORDER/general.ms nw?action=get_message&mview=0&ID_Message=45353

"This is where the narcissist differs from others (from 'normal' people). His very self is a piece of fiction concocted to fend off hurt and to nurture the narcissist's grandiosity. He fails in his 'reality test' - the ability to distinguish the actual from the imagined. The narcissist fervently believes in his own infallibility, brilliance, omnipotence, heroism, and perfection. He doesn't dare confront the truth and admit it even to himself."

The Narcissist's Confabulated Life - Sam Vaknin
http://samvak.tripod.com/journal75.html

"Narcissists are never whole without an adoring, submissive, self-denigrating partner. 'The victim's gullibility, selective blindness, malignant optimism are the weapons of the narcissist', says Vaknin."

Mirror, Mirror - Joanne Richard, Toronto Sun
http://www.canoe.ca/NewsStand/TorontoSun/Lifestyle/2004/08/30/608650.html

"By far the most authoritative and widely used instrument is the Millon Clinical Multiaxial Inventory-III (MCMI-III) - a potent test for personality disorders and attendant anxiety and depression. The third edition was formulated in 1996 by Theodore Millon and Roger Davis and includes 175 items. As many abusers show narcissistic traits, it is advisable to universally administer to them the Narcissistic Personality Inventory (NPI) as well."

Testing the Abuser -Sam Vaknin
http://samvak.tripod.com/abusefamily9.html

"By playing on the narcissist's grandiosity and paranoia, it is possible to deceive and manipulate him effortlessly. Just offer him Narcissistic Supply - admiration, affirmation, adulation - and he is yours. Harp on his insecurities and his persecutory delusions - and he is likely to trust only you and cling to you for dear life."

Abusing the Gullible Narcissist - Sam Vaknin
http://samvak.tripod.com/journal68.html

"'Who's the fairest of them all?' - asks the Bad Queen in the fairy tale. Having provided the wrong answer, the mirror is smashed to smithereens. Not a bad allegory for how the narcissist treats his 'friends'."

Dr. Watson and Mr. Hastings - The Narcissist and His Friends
- Sam Vaknin
http://www.narcissistic-abuse.com/journal85.html

"For her traumatic wounds to heal, the victim of abuse requires closure – one final interaction with her tormentor in which he, hopefully, acknowledges his misbehaviour and even tenders an apology. Fat chance."

The Three Forms of Closure - Sam Vaknin
http://www.narcissistic-abuse.com/abuse17.html

"There is no way to predict the longevity of any single relationship. It will last as long as the narcissist wants it to last, as long as he is deriving Narcissistic Supply, and as long as he hasn't found a new, 'better', Source of Supply."

Weekly Case Study - Sam Vaknin
http://groups.msn.com/NARCISSISTICPERSONALITYDISORDER/drvakninsweeklycasestudies.msnw
http://groups.msn.com/NARCISSISTICPERSONALITYDISORDER/drvakninsweeklycasestudies2.msnw

"Narcissists fear intimacy and they dread their deep-buried emotions. They are afraid to lose control. They regard a close, intimate, relationship as a threat and run away from it. You were dumped because you got too close for comfort."

Ask Sam Vaknin (Part II)
http://groups.msn.com/NARCISSISTICPERSONALITYDISORDER/general.msnw?action=get_message&mview=0&ID_Message=45353

"Question: I met many narcissists who are modest – even self-effacing. This seems to conflict with your observations. How do you reconcile the two?

Answer: The 'modesty' displayed by narcissists is false. It is mostly and merely verbal. It is couched in flourishing phrases, emphasised to absurdity, repeated unnecessarily – usually to the point of causing gross inconvenience to the listener. The real aim of such behaviour and its subtext are exactly the opposite of common modesty.

It is intended to either aggrandise the narcissist or to protect his grandiosity from scrutiny and possible erosion. Such modest outbursts precede inflated, grandiosity-laden statements made by the narcissist and pertaining to fields of human knowledge and activity in which he is sorely lacking. Devoid of systematic and methodical education, the narcissist tries to make do with pompous, or aggressive mannerisms, bombastic announcements, and the unnecessary and wrong usage of professional jargon. He attempts to dazzle his surroundings with apparent 'brilliance' and to put possible critics on the defence."

False Modesty - Sam Vaknin
http://samvak.tripod.com/faq36.html

"I equate love with weakness. I hate being weak and I hate and despise weak people (and, by implication, the very old and the very young). I do not tolerate stupidity, disease and dependence - and love seems to encompass all three. These are not sour grapes. I really feel this way."

My Woman and I - Sam Vaknin
http://samvak.tripod.com/journal3.html

"The dissolution of the abuser's marriage or other meaningful (romantic, business, or other) relationships constitutes a major life crisis and a scathing narcissistic injury. To soothe and salve the pain of disillusionment, he administers to his aching soul a mixture of lies, distortions, half-truths and outlandish interpretations of events around him."

The Relief of Being Abandoned - Sam Vaknin
http://samvak.tripod.com/abuse14.html

"Still, most abusers master the art of deception. People often find themselves involved with a abuser (emotionally, in business, or otherwise) before they have a chance to discover his real nature. When the abuser reveals his true colours, it is usually far too late. His victims are unable to separate from him. They are frustrated by this acquired helplessness and angry that they failed to see through the abuser earlier on."

The Tocsins of Abuse - The Abuser's Body Language - Sam Vaknin
http://samvak.tripod.com/abuse8.html

"The narcissist is confident that people find him irresistible. His unfailing charm is part of his self-imputed omnipotence. This inane conviction is what makes the narcissist a 'pathological charmer'. The somatic narcissist and the histrionic flaunt their sex appeal, virility or femininity, sexual prowess, musculature, physique, training, or athletic achievements. The cerebral narcissist seeks to enchant and entrance his audience with intellectual pyrotechnics. Many narcissists brag about their wealth, health, possessions, collections, spouses, children, personal history, family tree – in short: anything that garners them attention and renders them alluring."

The Pathological Charmer - Sam Vaknin
http://samvak.tripod.com/case05.html

"Moderator: So it is possible to have a narcissistic episode without having it your whole life?
  Vaknin: Opinions differ. In 1996 Gunderson reported that 'short term' NPD (up to three years) have been observed. Also, there is 'reactive narcissism' – following a major emotional injury or life crisis people tend to react by becoming more 'narcissistic'. But these are NOT the malignant forms I am dealing with in my book."

WebMD Chat Transcript with Sam Vaknin
http://my.webmd.com/content/article/71/81306.htm

"The narcissist is goal-orientated. Like a sophisticated cruise missile it homes in on Sources of Narcissistic Supply, 'conquers' them, conditions and moulds them and proceeds to extract from them attention, adulation, admiration and affirmation. This process demands the persistent investment of inordinate amounts of energy and time. The narcissist appears to be hell-bent, obsessed, smitten and addicted to the pursuit of his Sources of Supply. Yet, a curious transformation occurs once he has secured and 'chained' them. The narcissist – often abruptly – loses all interest."

Losing for Granted - Sam Vaknin
http://samvak.tripod.com/journal61.html

"Samuel Vaknin writes: The narcissist derives his sense of being, his experience of his own existence, and his self-worth from the outside. He mines others for Narcissistic Supply – adulation, attention, reflection, fear. Their reactions stalk his furnace. Absent Narcissistic Supply - the narcissist disintegrates and self - annihilates. When unnoticed, he feels empty and worthless. The narcissist MUST delude himself into believing that he is persistently the focus and object of the attentions, intentions, plans, feelings, and stratagems of other people. The narcissist faces a stark choice - either be (or become) the permanent centre of the world, or cease to be altogether."

>Ibid., p. 95, Narcissism and the Dynamics of Evil - D. McManaman
>http://learnv.ycdsb.edu.on.ca/lt/FMMC/hpteacher.nsf/Files/mcmanad/$FILE/narc.html

"Yet, one dose of Narcissistic Supply is enough to elevate the narcissists from the depth of misery to the heights of manic euphoria."

>Misdiagnosing Narcissism - The Bipolar I Disorder - Sam Vaknin
>http://samvak.tripod.com/journal71.html

"The narcissist 'knows' that he can do anything he chooses to do and excel in it. What the narcissist does, what he excels at, what he achieves, depends only on his volition. To his mind, there is no other determinant. Hence his rage when confronted with disagreement or opposition - not only because of the audacity of his, evidently inferior, adversaries. But because it threatens his world view, it endangers his feeling of omnipotence. The narcissist is often fatuously daring, adventurous, experimentative and curious precisely due to this hidden assumption of 'can-do'. He is genuinely surprised and devastated when he fails, when the 'Universe' does not arrange itself, magically, to accommodate his unbounded fantasies, when it (and people in it) does not comply with his whims and wishes."

>Grandiose Fantasies - Sam Vaknin
>http://samvak.tripod.com/faq3.html

"Question: Is there an ideal Source of Supply?

Answer: Of course there is (from the narcissist's point of view). The ideal Source of Supply is sufficiently intelligent to qualify as such, sufficiently gullible, submissive, reasonably (but not overly) inferior to the narcissist, has a good memory (with which to regulate the flow of Narcissistic Supply), available but not imposing, not explicitly or overtly manipulative, interchangeable (not indispensable), not demanding (a fatalist to a degree), attractive (if the narcissist is somatic). In short: a Galathea-Pygmallion type."

Excerpts from the Archives of the Narcissism List - Part 24 - Sam Vaknin
http://samvak.tripod.com/archive24.html

"Most narcissists I know – myself included – are misogynists. Their sexual and emotional lives are perturbed and chaotic. They are unable to love in any true sense of the word – nor are they capable of developing any measure of intimacy. Lacking empathy, they are incapable of offering to the partner emotional sustenance."

My Woman and I - Sam Vaknin
http://samvak.tripod.com/journal3.html

"The narcissist teams up with his partner because he regards IT as a Source of Narcissistic Supply. He values the partner as such a source. Put differently: the minute the partner ceases to supply him with what he needs – the narcissist loses all interest in IT. (I use IT judiciously – the narcissist objectifies his partners, he treats them as he would inanimate objects.)"

Getting Better - Sam Vaknin
http://samvak.tripod.com/faq12.html

Return

Links and Resources

[Abuse Resources](#)

[Interviews and Chats](#)

[Psychological Tests](#)

[Support Groups and Discussion, and Study Lists](#)

[Therapist Directories](#)

[Tutorials and Study Modules](#)

[Resources](#)

Abuse Resources
Articles and links related to abusive relationships.

Abusive Relationships FAQ
Frequently Asked Questions regarding abuse in relationships and how to cope with it.

Family Violence
Open Encyclopaedia entries about family violence and abuse.

Grant Me Serenity
A directory of resources for recovery from addictions, anxiety, and abuse.

Mental Health and Abuse
Various authors on forms of abuse, abusive relationships and coping methods.

Narcissism and Abusive Relationships Newsletter Archive
Abusive relationships Newsletter Archive – The Narcissistic Personality Disorder and abusive relationships with narcissists.

Narcissism, Narcissists, and Abusive Relationships
Bloc about pathological narcissism, the Narcissistic Personality Disorder (NPD), and abuse in relationships with narcissists and psychopaths.

Narcissistic Abusers in Relationships
Psychological profiles of abusers and their conduct in various relationships.

Open Directory Psychological Abuse
Directory of links to resources about psychological, verbal, and emotional abuse.

Rick A. Ross Institute
A database of information about cults, destructive cults, controversial groups and movements.

Sanctuary for the Abused
Resources, articles, blogs, and poetry for the abused.

Spousal and Domestic Abuse
Articles, links, discussions, and resources regarding spousal abuse and domestic violence.

Verbal and Emotional Abuse
Verbal, emotional and psychological abuse resources, articles, and discussions.

Women Abuse
Educating those who have a friend or family member in an abusive situation, or who are in an abusive relationship.

Interviews and Chats

Interviews and chats regarding the Narcissistic Personality Disorder and abusive relationships.

Mental Health Today Narcissistic PD Chat Transcript
Narcissistic Personality Disorder chat transcript – abusive relationships, divorce, idealisation and devaluation, strategies or coping.

Mirror, Mirror
Article in "Toronto Sun" about malignant narcissists in various settings (mainly the family and the workplace).

Narcissism Radio Show
Hour long radio show about the Narcissistic Personality Disorder, abuse in relationships with narcissists, and listeners call-ins.

Narcissistic Personality Disorder Audio Interview
Audio interview with Sam Vaknin regarding the Narcissistic Personality Disorder - clinical and cultural aspects.

Narcissistic Personality Disorder Chat
Chat regarding the Narcissistic Personality Disorder and pathological narcissism.

Narcissists in the Workplace
Chat transcript regarding narcissists in the workplace and how to cope with them.

Narcissists, Group Behaviour, and Terrorism
Pathological narcissism and its incidence in various ethnic, religious, or professional groups as well as its connection to terrorism and violent crime.

New Narc City
Narcissism as manifested in various social institutions - from Wall Street to the Catholic Church.

Psychopaths in Suits
Psychopaths in management and in positions of corporate authority - transcript of ABC Radio National's Background Briefing.

Relationships with Abusive Narcissists Chat Transcript
Transcript of chat regarding abusive narcissists and their victims.

The Ambassador of Narcissism
An interview in Natterbox with Sam Vaknin, author of "Malignant Self Love - Narcissism Revisited".

The Infinite Mind - Narcissism
Interviews with mental health professionals, narcissists, and artists about the disorder and its implications.

WebMD Chat - Narcissistic Personality Disorder
A WebMD chat about the Narcissistic Personality Disorder with Sam Vaknin, author of "Malignant Self Love - Narcissism Revisited".

Psychological Tests
Psychological testing and online psychological tests with emphasis on personality testing.

American Psychological Association Psychological Testing
The authoritative guide to psychological testing, including online psychological testing.

Hypersensitive Narcissism Scale
Online copy and interpretation of the Hypersensitive Narcissism Scale (HSNS).

My Therapy
Subscription only online psychological diagnosis and testing.

Narcissistic Personality Inventory
A test is made up of 223 items (pairs of statements)that sample the domain of the narcissistic personality.

Online Psychological Tests
Online personality tests - a directory of links from Yahoo!

Online Psychological Tests Guide
The American Psychological Association's online psychological testing Web guide.

Pearson Assessments
Dozens of commercially available mental health diagnostic tests, including the MMPI-II and the Millon Clinical Inventories.

Personality Disorders Tests
Tests to diagnose personality disorders.

Psychological Testing
Psychological online and offline test and a guide to psychological testing. Includes a therapist directory.

Psychological Tests
A directory of links to psychological tests on the Web (especially personality, emotional intelligence, and relationship tests).

Psychotherapeutic Assessment of NPD
Psychotherapeutic Assessment and Treatment of Narcissistic Personality Disorder from the American Psychiatric Association.

PsychTests
Free online psychological evaluation and assessment tests.

Structured Clinical Interview (SCID)
Diagnostic interview designed to assist clinicians, researchers, and trainees in making reliable DSM-IV psychiatric diagnoses.

4degreez Personality Disorder Test
An online personality disorder test from 4degreez.

Support Groups and Discussion, and Study Lists

Support Groups and Discussion, and Study Lists regarding the Narcissistic Personality Disorder.

Abuse by Narcissists Study List
Abuse by malignant narcissists - a daily dose of articles, essays, studies and links selected from hundreds of resources.

Toxic Relationships Study List
Abusive and toxic relationships in a variety of settings (marriage, workplace, etc.) – characteristics, tips, and advice.

Adult Children Of Narcissists
Group is for adult children of narcissistic parents.

Adults Recovering From Narcissistic Parents
Support group for changing old behaviours which hinder the healthy development of children of Narcissists.

Beyond the Echo
Recovery for adults coming from a dysfunctional narcissistic family of origin.

Children of Narcissistic Personality Disorder Forum
Support and discussion forum for children of malignant narcissists.

Coping with the Psychopath/Narcissist Child
Coping with a child diagnosed with a Narcissistic or Antisocial Personality Disorder.

Echo's Reply
Internet community lending support to those persons who, have survived a relationship with and/or are still coping with individuals suffering from NPD (Narcissistic Personality Disorder).

Narcex – Single Parenting with a Narcissist
Discussion group for ex-spouses or separated co-parents of narcissists.

Narcissistic Personality Disorder Forum
A Mental Health Today Forum to discuss the Narcissistic Personality Disorder and pathological narcissism.

Narcissism FAQ Farm
Questions and answers regarding the various dimensions of pathological narcissism.

Narcissist's Support Group
E-mail support group for individuals with narcissistic behaviour or have NPD.

Narcissistic Escape
Forum for discussing narcissistic abuse and the aftermath of a narcissistic relationship.

Narcissistic Personality Disorder
Resources, learning, and discussion group for people who maintain relationships with abusive narcissists.

Narcissistic Personality Disorder Discussion and Support Group
Discussion and support group for people affected by the Narcissistic Personality Disorder, their spouses, colleagues, families, and friends.

Narcissistic Personality Disorder Group
Article announcements and study of pathological narcissism and abuse in relationships.

Narcissistic Personality Disorder List
A discussion and support group for victims of abuse by narcissists.

Narcissistic Personality Family Forum
Support and discussion forum for families of narcissists.

Narcissistic Support Group
Support group for the victims of narcissism and the sufferers of Narcissistic Personality Disorder (NPD).

N-Magnets Anonymous
Discussion and support group dedicated to the victims of narcissists.

N-Partners Disorder Support
Support and discussion group for sufferers of the Echo Personality Disorder ("Inverted Narcissism").

People Pleasers
Resources and support group for people pleasers who fall prey to narcissists.

PsychForums NPD Support Community
PsychForums Narcissistic Personality Disorder support community.

Psychopath Support and Study Group
Support group, resources, and forum for victims of psychopaths.

Safe and Secure
Support group for survivors of partners/parents/coworkers with Narcissistic Personality Disorder.

Support Groups FOR NARCISSISTS
Support groups for people diagnosed with the Narcissistic Personality Disorder (NPD), or with narcissistic traits, style, and personality.

The Narcissism Announcement List
This list is not a support list. It is intended to study the causes, effects and manifestations of pathological narcissism. Contributions from members are welcome. The Narcissism List is an "Announcement List". Members of the list receive daily –

articles, book reviews, essays, analyses, literary pieces, Web addresses and many other materials relating to pathological narcissism and the Narcissistic Personality Disorder.

Voicelessness and Emotional Survival Message Board
A forum to discuss your experience with voicelessness and narcissism.

Catholics Living With Narcissists
Support group for Catholics living with people diagnosed with the Narcissistic Personality Disorder (NPD).

Therapist Directories

Therapist links and Web directories and find a therapist directories.

ABCs of Internet Therapy
Independent consumer guide to therapists and counselours who provide help over the Internet – compiled by consumers.

Consumers' Guide to Online Mental Health Care
Guidelines for selecting online mental health care providers and counselours as well as online databases.

Counselling Services on the Web
Psychological counselling and care giving services on the Web.

Get Mental Help
Listings of psychiatrists, psychologists, therapists, social workers, counselours, and other mental health practitioners.

More Therapist Directories
Additional online therapist directories from the Yahoo! Web directory.

Therapist Directories on the Web
A compressive list of all the therapist directories on the Web. Find therapists by specialisation (look for "personality disorders") and state or region.

Therapist Locator in the United States
Directory of marriage and family therapists.

Tutorials and Study Modules

Tutorials and Study Modules regarding the Narcissistic Personality Disorder (NPD).

Narcissism At Work
Slide presentation by Dattner Consulting regarding narcissism at work.

Resources

Information and research regarding the Narcissistic Personality Disorder (NPD).

Healthy Place – Personality Disorders – Narcissism
Narcissistic PD and abuse by narcissists – FAQs, essays, links, and book excerpts.

Malignant Self Love – Narcissism Revisited
A book-length essay, 102 frequently asked questions, excerpts from the Narcissism List and appendices regarding the Narcissistic Personality Disorder (NPD), relationships with abusive narcissists, and pathological narcissism.

Open Directory Narcissistic Personality Disorder Category
Links to pathological narcissism and Narcissistic Personality Disorder (NPD) resources on the Web.

The Serial Bully
Bullying and stalking correlated to psychological profiles and typology, including the Narcissistic Personality Disorder. Advice, useful addresses, on-line resources.

A Primer on Narcissism
An essay regarding the formation, characteristics, dynamics and inter-relationships of pathological narcissism.

Controlling Parents
The role of controlling parents in dysfunctional families – the breeding grounds of a host of personality disorders, including the Narcissistic Personality Disorder (NPD). Be sure to visit the links page.

Distinctions between Self-Esteem and Narcissism
A book sized essay regarding self-esteem as a goal of early childhood education, distinctions between self-esteem and narcissism and appropriate practices. Contains references and a bibliography.

Dual Diagnosis and Narcissism
A comprehensive overview of NPD, treatment options and dual diagnoses (mainly drug or alcohol abuse).

Holding the Mirror
The journal, reflections, and studies of an enabler of a narcissist. The anatomy of abuse explored with candour and astuteness.

Kathi's Mental Health Review – Narcissism
FAQs, book excerpts, and other resources regarding the Narcissistic Personality Disorder.

Mental Health Matters Narcissistic Personality Disorder
FAQs, recommended reading, and resources regarding the Narcissistic Personality Disorder (NPD) and abuse in relationships with narcissists.

Mental Health Net – Narcissistic Personality Disorder
The symptoms of the Narcissistic Personality Disorder (NPD), treatment modalities and on-line resources.

N-Courage Health Network
Definitions of types of narcissists, recovery, support, recommended reading and Internet resources.

Narcissism 101
Overview – from personal experience – of literature about pathological narcissism and the Narcissistic Personality Disorder (NPD).

Narcissism in the Boardroom
Two-part United Press International (UPI) essay about how pathological narcissism can explain many of the recent fraud-laced corporate scandals.

Narcissism: A Genetic Trait
Narcissism, violence and aggression might be hereditary. The NPA personality theory is presented.

Narcissism: A Nine Headed Hydra?
A typology of pathological narcissists with examples, recommended reading, advice, and case studies.

Narcissist Personality Disorder Directory
Articles, frequently asked questions, advice columns, support groups and Web and print resources concerned with the Narcissistic Personality Disorder.

Narcissistic Abuse Information
Manipulation, betrayal, lying, belittling, no empathy – information about narcissists and how to deal with them. Lists of recommended reading.

Narcissistic PD
Narcissistic Personality Disorder: FAQs, resources, books and information.

Narcissistic Personality Disorder
Encyclopaedia article about the Narcissistic Personality Disorder (NPD).

Narcissistic Personality Disorder
Information, resources, and case studies regarding ten personality disorders, including NPD.

Narcissistic Personality Disorder (NPD)
The Narcissistic Personality Disorder criteria, quotes from textbooks and links.

Narcissistic Personality Disorder Sanctuary
DSM-IV criteria, bookstore and recommended reading, resources, articles, and discussion and support boards.

Narcissistic Personality Disorder Today
Narcissistic Personality Disorder information, online resources, recommended reading, and support groups.

On Narcissistic Personality Disorders
The phrase "narcissistic personality disorders" on various search engines – news, multimedia, lists and off-Web.

Open Site Narcissistic Personality Disorder
DSM criteria and information regarding the Narcissistic Personality Disorder (NPD) and pathological narcissism.

Pathological Narcissism Primer and Glossary
Download a Pathological Narcissism and Narcissistic Personality Disorder (NPD) Primer and Glossary covering more than 100 topics in depth (Babylon browser required).

Perfectly Flawed – The Anatomy of a Failed Narcissist
The personal voyage of a narcissist faced with his debilitating disorder.

PTypes Personality Disorders
Personality disorders and personality types correlated using the Briggs-Myers typology. Lists of resources, famous people with personality disorders, links. Especially important are the discussions of the narcissistic, compensatory narcissistic, inventive, borderline, and mercurial personalities.

Report of a Quest
Pathological narcissism as the defence mechanism underlying paraphilias.

So, You are in Love with a Narcissist
Articles about falling in love and leaving a narcissist.

The Maccoby Group
Narcissism and leadership in corporate settings – articles, research projects and resources.

The Narcissistic Bully
Psychological abuse, narcissism, and relationships.

The Weaver and Narcissist
The main traits of pathological narcissism, splitting, and other primitive defense mechanisms.

Theodore Millon on Narcissism
Theodore Millon's seminal chapter on pathological narcissism in his book "Disorders of Personality".

Voicelessness: Narcissism
Narcissism and narcissistic disorders described and analysed from the point of view of the voicelessness paradigm developed by Dr. Richard Grossman.

What Makes Narcissists Tick
Why malignant narcissists behave the way they do, with examples of narcissistic behaviour.

Who's the Fairest of Them All?
A doctoral dissertation regarding the impact of narcissism on self- and other- rated fairness in the workplace.

Wikipedia on Narcissism
Encyclopaedia entry about the psychodynamics of pathological narcissism.

Narcissistic Personality Disorder (NPD)
The Narcissistic Personality Disorder described, recommended readings, referral to discussion and support groups - with emphasis on the outcomes of narcissistic behaviour and their impact on others.

Narcissism Info
Narcissism information, frequently asked questions, and forum

Personality Disorders on Suite101
Articles, blog, and discussions regarding personality disorders.

Tips of All Sorts - Narcissism
Tips, advice, resources, and recommended reading on how to cope with malignant narcissists

Tips of All Sorts - Abusive Relationships
Tips, advice, resources, and recommended reading on how to cope with abusers in all kinds of abusive relationships.

Tips of All Sorts - Coping with a Paranoid Ex-spouse
Tips, advice, resources, and recommended reading on how to cope with a paranoid ex-spouse.

Tips of All Sorts - Coping with Stalking and Stalkers

Tips, advice, resources, and recommended reading on how to cope with a stalker.

Tips of All Sorts - Divorcing a Narcissist or a Psychopath
Tips, advice, resources, and recommended reading on how to divorce a narcissist or a psychopath.
Tips of All Sorts - Workplace Bully
Tips, advice, resources, and recommended reading on how to copy with a workplace bully.
On Narcissism
An essay regarding pathological narcissism, narcissistic disorders, treatment and prognosis.

Return

Born in 1961 in Qiryat-Yam, Israel.

Served in the Israeli Defence Force (1979-1982) in training and education units.

Education

1970-1978: Completed nine semesters in the Technion – Israel Institute of Technology, Haifa.

1982-3: Ph.D. in Philosophy (dissertation: "Time Asymmetry Revisited") – Pacific Western University, **California**, USA.

1982-5: Graduate of numerous courses in Finance Theory and International Trading in the UK and USA.

Certified E-Commerce Concepts Analyst by Brainbench.

Certified in Psychological Counselling Techniques by Brainbench.

Certified Financial Analyst by Brainbench.

Full proficiency in Hebrew and in English.

Business Experience

1980 to 1983

Founder and co-owner of a chain of computerised information kiosks in Tel-Aviv, Israel.

1982 to 1985

Senior positions with the Nessim D. Gaon Group of Companies in Geneva, Paris and New-York (NOGA and APROFIM SA):

– Chief Analyst of Edible Commodities in the Group's Headquarters in Switzerland
– Manager of the Research and Analysis Division
– Manager of the Data Processing Division
– Project Manager of the Nigerian Computerised Census
– Vice President in charge of RND and Advanced Technologies
– Vice President in charge of Sovereign Debt Financing

1985 to 1986

Represented Canadian Venture Capital Funds in Israel.

1986 to 1987

General Manager of IPE Ltd. in London. The firm financed international multi-lateral countertrade and leasing transactions.

1988 to 1990

Co-founder and Director of "Mikbats-Tesuah", a portfolio management firm based in Tel-Aviv. Activities included large-scale portfolio management, underwriting, forex trading and general financial advisory services.

1990 to Present

Freelance consultant to many of Israel's Blue-Chip firms, mainly on issues related to the capital markets in Israel, Canada, the UK and the USA.

Consultant to foreign RND ventures and to Governments on macro-economic matters.

Freelance journalist in various media in the United States.

1990 to 1995

President of the Israel chapter of the Professors World Peace Academy (PWPA) and (briefly) Israel representative of the "Washington Times".

1993 to 1994

Co-owner and Director of many business enterprises:

– The Omega and Energy Air-Conditioning Concern
– AVP Financial Consultants
– Handiman Legal Services
   Total annual turnover of the group: 10 million USD.

Co-owner, Director and Finance Manager of COSTI Ltd. – Israel's largest computerised information vendor and developer. Raised funds through a series of private placements locally in the USA, Canada and London.

1993 to 1996

Publisher and Editor of a Capital Markets Newsletter distributed by subscription only to dozens of subscribers countrywide.

In a legal precedent in 1995 – studied in business schools and law faculties across Israel – was tried for his role in an attempted takeover of Israel's Agriculture Bank.

Was interned in the State School of Prison Wardens.

Managed the Central School Library, wrote, published and lectured on various occasions.

Managed the Internet and International News Department of an Israeli mass media group, "Ha-Tikshoret and Namer".

Assistant in the Law Faculty in Tel-Aviv University (to Prof. S.G. Shoham).

1996 to 1999

Financial consultant to leading businesses in Macedonia, Russia and the Czech Republic.

Economic commentator in "Nova Makedonija", "Dnevnik", "Makedonija Denes", "Izvestia", "Argumenti i Fakti", "The Middle East Times", "The New Presence", "Central Europe Review", and other periodicals, and in the economic programs on various channels of Macedonian Television.

Chief Lecturer in courses in Macedonia organised by the Agency of Privatization, by the Stock Exchange, and by the Ministry of Trade.

1999 to 2002

Economic Advisor to the Government of the Republic of Macedonia and to the Ministry of Finance.

2001 to 2003

Senior Business Correspondent for United Press International (UPI).

2007 -

Associate Editor, Global Politician

Founding Analyst, The Analyst Network

Contributing Writer, The American Chronicle Media Group

Expert, Self-growth.com

2007-2008

Columnist and analyst in "Nova Makedonija", "Fokus", and "Kapital" (Macedonian papers and newsweeklies).

2008-

Member of the Steering Committee for the Advancement of Healthcare in the Republic of Macedonia

Advisor to the Minister of Health of Macedonia

Seminars and lectures on economic issues in various forums in Macedonia.

Web and Journalistic Activities

Author of extensive Web sites in:

– Psychology ("Malignant Self Love") - An Open Directory Cool Site for 8 years.

– Philosophy ("Philosophical Musings"),

– Economics and Geopolitics ("World in Conflict and Transition").

Owner of the Narcissistic Abuse Study Lists and the Abusive Relationships Newsletter (more than 6,000 members).

Owner of the Economies in Conflict and Transition Study List , the Toxic Relationships Study List, and the Links and Factoid Study List.

Editor of mental health disorders and Central and Eastern Europe categories in various Web directories (Open Directory, Search Europe, Mentalhelp.net).

Editor of the Personality Disorders, Narcissistic Personality Disorder, the Verbal and Emotional Abuse, and the Spousal (Domestic) Abuse and Violence topics on Suite 101 and Bellaonline.

Columnist and commentator in "The New Presence", United Press International (UPI), InternetContent, eBookWeb, PopMatters, Global Politician, The Analyst Network, Conservative Voice, The American Chronicle Media Group, eBookNet.org, and "Central Europe Review".

Publications and Awards

"Managing Investment Portfolios in States of Uncertainty", Limon Publishers, Tel-Aviv, 1988

"The Gambling Industry", Limon Publishers, Tel-Aviv, 1990

"Requesting My Loved One – Short Stories", Yedioth Aharonot, Tel-Aviv, 1997

"The Suffering of Being Kafka" (electronic book of Hebrew and English Short Fiction), Prague, 1998-2004

"The Macedonian Economy at a Crossroads – On the Way to a Healthier Economy" (dialogues with Nikola Gruevski), Skopje, 1998

"The Exporters' Pocketbook", Ministry of Trade, Republic of Macedonia, Skopje, 1999

"Malignant Self Love – Narcissism Revisited", Narcissus Publications, Prague, 1999-2007 (Read excerpts - click here)

The Narcissism, Psychopathy, and Abuse in Relationships Series
(E-books regarding relationships with abusive narcissists and psychopaths), Prague, 1999-2010

Personality Disorders Revisited (e-book about personality disorders), Prague, 2007

"After the Rain – How the West Lost the East", Narcissus Publications in association with Central Europe Review/CEENMI, Prague and Skopje, 2000

Winner of numerous awards, among them Israel's Council of Culture and Art Prize for Maiden Prose (1997), The Rotary Club Award for Social Studies (1976), and the Bilateral Relations Studies Award of the American Embassy in Israel (1978).

Hundreds of professional articles in all fields of finance and economics, and numerous articles dealing with geopolitical and political economic issues published in both print and Web periodicals in many countries.

Many appearances in the electronic media on subjects in philosophy and the sciences, and concerning economic matters.

Write to Me:
palma@unet.com.mk
narcissisticabuse-owner@yahoogroups.com

My Web Sites:

Economy/Politics:
http://ceeandbalkan.tripod.com/

Psychology:
http://www.narcissistic-abuse.com/

Philosophy:
http://philosophos.tripod.com/

Poetry:
http://samvak.tripod.com/contents.html

Fiction:
http://samvak.tripod.com/sipurim.html

Return

Abused? Stalked? Harassed? Bullied? Victimized?
Afraid? Confused? Need HELP? DO SOMETHING ABOUT IT!

Had a Narcissistic Parent?
Married to a Narcissist – or Divorcing One?
Afraid your children will turn out the same?
Want to cope with this pernicious, baffling condition?
OR
Are You a Narcissist – or suspect that You are one...
This book will teach you how to...
Cope, Survive, and Protect Your Loved Ones!
You should read...

"Malignant Self Love – Narcissism Revisited"
The EIGHTH, REVISED PRINTING (January 2007) is now available!

Nine additional e-books, All NEW Editions, JUST RELEASED!!!
Malignant Self Love, Toxic Relationships,
Pathological Narcissism, Coping with Divorce,
The Narcissist and Psychopath in the Workplace – and MORE!!!

Click on this link to purchase the PRINT BOOK and/or
the NINE E-BOOKS
http://www.narcissistic-abuse.com/thebook.html

Sam Vaknin published the EIGHTH, REVISED IMPRESSION of his book about relationships with abusive narcissists, **"Malignant Self Love – Narcissism Revisited"**.

The book deals with the Narcissistic Personality Disorder and its effects on the narcissist and his nearest and dearest – in 102 frequently asked questions and two essays – a total of 600 pages!

Print Edition from BARNES AND NOBLE and AMAZON

Barnes and Noble – "Malignant Self Love – Narcissism Revisited" EIGHTH, Revised, Impression (January 2007)

ON SALE starting at $40.45 !!!

INSTEAD OF the publisher's list price of $54.95 (including shipping and handling)!!!

That's more than $14 off the publisher's list price!!!!

Click on this link to purchase the paper edition:

http://search.barnesandnoble.com/bookSearch/isbnInquiry.asp?r=1&ISBN=9788023833843

And from **Amazon.com** – Click on this link:

http://www.amazon.com/exec/obidos/tg/detail/-/8023833847/

Print Edition from the PUBLISHER

The previous revised impression of Sam Vaknin's "Malignant Self – Love – Narcissism Revisited".

Comes with an exclusive BONUS PACK (not available through Barnes and Noble or Amazon).

Contains the entire text: essays, frequently asked questions and appendices regarding pathological narcissism and the Narcissistic Personality Disorder (NPD).

The publisher charges the full list price – but throws into the bargain a bonus pack with hundreds of additional pages and seven free e-books.

Click on this link:

http://www.ccnow.com/cgi-local/cart.cgi?vaksam_MSL

Free excerpts from the EIGHTH, Revised Impression of **"Malignant Self Love - Narcissism Revisited"** are available as well as a free NEW EDITION of the Narcissism Book of Quotes

Click on this link to download the files:

http://www.narcissistic-abuse.com/freebooks.html

"After the Rain - How the West Lost the East"

The history, cultures, societies, and economies of countries in transition in the Balkans.

Click on this link to purchase this print book:

http://www.ccnow.com/cgi-local/cart.cgi?vaksam_ATR

Electronic Books (e-books) from the Publisher

An *electronic book* is a computer file, sent to you as an attachment to an e-mail message. Just save it to your hard disk and click on the file to open, read, and learn!

1. **"Malignant Self Love - Narcissism Revisited"**
   Eighth, Revised Edition (January 2007)

The e-book version of Sam Vaknin's "Malignant Self - Love - Narcissism Revisited". Contains the entire text: essays, frequently asked questions (FAQs) and appendices regarding pathological narcissism and the Narcissistic Personality Disorder (NPD).

Click on this link to purchase the e-book:

http://www.ccnow.com/cgi-local/cart.cgi?vaksam_MSL-EBOOK

2. **"The Narcissism, Psychopathy, and Abuse in Relationships Series"** Eighth, Revised Edition (July 2010)

NINE e-books (more than 3000 pages), including the full text of "Malignant Self Love - Narcissism Revisited", regarding Pathological Narcissism, relationships with abusive narcissists and psychopaths, and the Narcissistic Personality Disorder (NPD).

Click on this link to purchase the EIGHT e-books:

http://www.ccnow.com/cgi-local/cart.cgi?vaksam_SERIES

3. **"Toxic Relationships - Abuse and its Aftermath"**
   Fourth Edition (February 2006)

   How to identify abuse, cope with it, survive it, and deal with your abuser and with the system in divorce and custody issues.

   Click on this link to purchase the e-book:

   http://www.ccnow.com/cgi-local/cart.cgi?vaksam_ABUSE

4. **"The Narcissist and Psychopath in the Workplace"**
   (September 2006)

   Identify abusers, bullies, and stalkers in the workplace (bosses, colleagues, suppliers, and authority figures) and learn how to cope with them effectively.

   Click on this link to purchase the e-book:

   http://www.ccnow.com/cgi-local/cart.cgi?vaksam_WORKPLACE

5. **"Abusive Relationships Workbook"** (February 2006)

   Self-assessment questionnaires, tips, and tests for victims of abusers, batterers, and stalkers in various types of relationships.

   Click on this link to purchase the e-book:

   http://www.ccnow.com/cgi-local/cart.cgi?vaksam_WORKBOOK

6. **"Pathological Narcissism FAQs"**
   Eighth, Revised Edition (January 2007)

   Dozens of Frequently Asked Questions regarding Pathological Narcissism, relationships with abusive narcissists, and the Narcissistic Personality Disorder.

   Click on this link to purchase the e-book:

   http://www.ccnow.com/cgi-local/cart.cgi?vaksam_FAQS

7. **"The World of the Narcissist"**
   Eighth, Revised Edition (January 2007)

   A book-length psychodynamic study of pathological narcissism, relationships with abusive narcissists, and the Narcissistic Personality Disorder, using a new vocabulary.

   Click on this link to purchase the e-book:

   http://www.ccnow.com/cgi-local/cart.cgi?vaksam_ESSAY

8. **"Excerpts from the Archives of the Narcissism List"**

Hundreds of excerpts from the archives of the Narcissistic Abuse Study List regarding Pathological Narcissism, relationships with abusive narcissists, and the Narcissistic Personality Disorder (NPD).

Click on this link to purchase the e-book:

http://www.ccnow.com/cgi-local/cart.cgi?vaksam_EXCERPTS

9. **"Diary of a Narcissist"** (November 2005)

The anatomy of one man's mental illness – its origins, its unfolding, its outcomes.

Click on this link to purchase the e-book:

http://www.ccnow.com/cgi-local/cart.cgi?vaksam_JOURNAL

10. *"The Narcissist and Psychopath in Therapy"*

Can narcissists and psychopaths be cured? Can their behaviour be modified? How are these mental health disorders diagnosed?

Buy it from the publisher - click on this link:

http://www.ccnow.com/cgi-local/cart.cgi?vaksam_THERAPY

11. "After the Rain - How the West Lost the East"

The history, cultures, societies, and economies of countries in transition in the Balkans.

Click on this link to purchase the e-book:

http://www.ccnow.com/cgi-local/cart.cgi?vaksam_ATR-EBOOK

Download Free Electronic Books

Click on this link:

http://www.narcissistic-abuse.com/freebooks.html

More about the Books and Additional Resources

The Eighth, Revised Impression (January 2007) of the Print Edition of **"Malignant Self Love - Narcissism Revisited"** includes:

- The full text of "Malignant Self Love - Narcissism Revisited"
- The full text of 102 Frequently Asked Questions and Answers

- Covering all the dimensions of Pathological Narcissism and Abuse in Relationships
- An Essay – The Narcissist's point of view
- Bibliography
- 600 printed pages in a quality paper book
- Digital Bonus Pack! (available only when you purchase the previous edition from the Publisher) – Bibliography, three e-books, additional FAQs, appendices and more – hundreds of additional pages!

Testimonials and Additional Resources

You can read Readers' Reviews at the Barnes and Noble Web page dedicated to "Malignant Self Love" – HERE:

http://search.barnesandnoble.com/bookSearch/isbnInquiry.asp?r=1&ISBN=9788023833843

Dozens of Links and Resources

Click on these links:

The Narcissistic Abuse Study List
http://groups.yahoo.com/group/narcissisticabuse

The Toxic Relationships Study List
http://groups.yahoo.com/group/toxicrelationships

Abusive Relationships Newsletter
http://groups.google.com/group/narcissisticabuse

Participate in Discussions about Abusive Relationships - click on these links:

http://narcissisticabuse.ning.com/

http://www.runboard.com/bnarcissisticabuserecovery

http://thepsychopath.freeforums.org/

The Narcissistic Abuse Study List

http://health.groups.yahoo.com/group/narcissisticabuse/

The Toxic Relationships Study List

http://groups.yahoo.com/group/toxicrelationships

Abusive Relationships Newsletter

http://groups.google.com/group/narcissisticabuse/

Archived discussion threads - click on these links:

http://personalitydisorders.suite101.com/discussions.cfm

http://www.suite101.com/discussions.cfm/verbal_emotional_abuse

http://www.suite101.com/discussuions.cfm/spousal_domestic_abuse

Links to Therapist Directories, Psychological Tests, NPD Resources, Support Groups for Narcissists and Their Victims, and Tutorials

http://health.groups.yahoo.com/group/narcissisticabuse/message/5458

Support Groups for Victims of Narcissists and Narcissists

http://dmoz.org/Health/Mental_Health/Disorders/Personality/Narcissistic

BE WELL, SAFE AND WARM WHEREVER YOU ARE!

Sam Vaknin

Made in the USA
Middletown, DE
14 May 2024